WITHDRAWN

Innocent

Fernando Bermudez. *Photo by Marc Wishengrad*

"Innocent"

Inside Wrongful Conviction Cases

Scott Christianson

NEW YORK UNIVERSITY PRESS
New York and London

For my parents,

Keith and Joyce Christianson

NEW YORK UNIVERSITY PRESS
New York and London
www.nyupress.org

© 2004 by Scott Christianson

Library of Congress Cataloging-in-Publication Data
Christianson, Scott.
Innocent : inside wrongful conviction cases / Scott Christianson.
p. cm.
Includes bibliographical references.
ISBN 0–8147–1634–2 (cloth : alk. paper)
1. Judicial error—United States—Cases.   2. Criminal justice,
Administration of—United States—Cases.   I. Title.
KF9756.C49 2004
345.73'05—dc22   2003016327

New York University Press books are printed on acid-free paper,
and their binding materials are chosen for strength and durability.

Manufactured in the United States of America

10 9 8 7 6 5 4 3 2 1

Contents

Acknowledgments

I am grateful to numerous individuals who spoke with me, on or off the record, about this topic. Special thanks are due to those described in these stories. Two legal organizations in particular provided special assistance. From the New York Defenders Association, which supported the research, the following persons were especially helpful: Jonathan E. Gradess, Barbara Baggott, Charlie O'Brien, Isaiah "Skip" Gant, Ken Strutin, Mardi Crawford, Tom Brewer, and Shahrul Ladue. From the Legal Aid Society of New York, Russell Neufeld, Sara Bennett, John Boston, Carey Elgarden, Susan Epstein, Rich Joselson, Andrew C. Fine, Michelle Fox, Bill Gibney, Nancy Little, Joanne Legano Ross, Lori Shellenberger, Steve Wasserman, and Cynthia Wolpert graciously shared their expertise and experiences and in some instances put me in contact with their clients and opened their case files to me.

From John Jay College of Criminal Justice, President Gerald Lynch, Dean Emeritus Hank Smit, and Jerry Capeci assisted with the companion exhibit. Assemblyman John J. McEneny sponsored the exhibit at the New York State Legislative Office Building. I am also grateful to the Puffin Foundation Ltd. for its generous support of the exhibition.

Many others helped provide valuable information and assistance, including Prof. James R. Acker, University at Albany; Prof. Anthony Amsterdam, New York University Law School; George H. Barber, former appeals chief, Albany County District Attorney's Office; former New York State administrative judge Richard Bartlett; Prof. Hugo A. Bedau, Tufts University; Myron Beldock of Beldock Levine and Hoffman; Fernando and Crystal Bermudez; Prof. Adele Bernhard, Pace

Law School; Prof. Leigh Bienen, Northwestern University, School of Law; Jeffrey Blake; Antoinette Bosco; Leonard Bourin, ABC News; Robert Boyle of New York; Stephen Braga, of Baker Botts, L.L.P., Washington, D.C.; Paul W. Browne, assistant commissioner, New York Police Department; Sean Byrne, New York Prosecutors Training Institute; Walter Chattman, New York State Department of Correctional Services; Priscilla Read Chenoweth and Lesley Chenoweth Estevao; Prof. Paul Chevigny, New York University Law School; Prof. Bell Chevigny; Simon F. Cole, Cornell University; Alison Coleman, Prison Families of New York; Phyllis Collazo, *The New York Times*; Assemblyman Samuel Colman, District 93; Gary Craig, Rochester *Democrat and Chronicle*; Rosaleen Crotty; Chuck Culhane; Mary Ann DiBari; Richard Dieter, Death Penalty Information Center; Kevin M. Doyle, New York State capital defender; Karen Draves, Prisoners Legal Services of New York; Jim Dwyer, *The New York Times*; Jethro M. Eisenstein; Ethical Culture Society of New York; Eddie Ellis; Richard Emery; David Feige, Bronx Defenders; Daniel Feldman, New York State assistant attorney general; Kevin Flynn, *The New York Times*; Tom Flynn, Rochester *Democrat and Chronicle*; Prof. Eric M. Freedman, Hofstra University School of Law; Joel Freedman; Assemblyman David Gantt, District 133; Mickey Garcia; Jon Getz, Rochester attorney; Paul Gianelli, Hauppauge attorney; Eleanor Goldsmith; Jennifer Gonnerman, *Village Voice*; Neil Gordon, Center for Public Integrity, Washington, D.C.; Robert Gottlieb; Dr. Alice Green, Center for Law and Justice; Norman L. Greene, Association of the Bar of the City of New York; Prof. Samuel R. Gross, University of Michigan Law School; Lawrence Halfond, Esq., of Queens; Denis Hamill, New York *Daily News*; Charles Hamilton, Iris Hamilton, and Barbara Hamilton; Curtis Harris, *City Limits*; Mark Harris, New York State deputy capital defender; Prof. William E. Hellerstein, Brooklyn Law School; Jack S. Hoffinger, Hoffinger, Friedland Dobrish and Stern; Cheri Hunter, New York County District Attorney's Office; Patsy Kelly Jarrett; Judge John Keenan, Southern District of New York; Richard Jacoby; David Kaczynski of New Yorkers Against the Death Penalty; Aliza B. Kaplan of the Innocence Project at Cardozo Law School, Yeshiva University; Bill Kennedy and Don Faulkner of the New York State Writers Institute; Terry Kindlon of Kindlon and Shanks in

Albany; Daryl King; David Klingaman, chief clerk, New York State Court of Claims; Ron Kuby of the Center for Constitutional Rights; Gregory Lasak, Queens District Attorney's Office; Prof. Richard Leo, University of California at Irvine; Prof. James Liebman, Columbia Law School; Superintendent Elaine Lord, Bedford Hills Correctional Facility; Mark Mahoney, Buffalo attorney; John Martin, ABC News; Marcy Marzuki, Swell Productions, Chicago; Charlita Mays of Richards, Spears, Kibbe and Orbe; Rev. Jim McCloskey and staff, Centurion Ministries, Princeton, New Jersey; Marianne McClure; Emel McDowell; Robert Meeropol, Rosenberg Fund for Children; Holly Murdoch, Actuality Productions; Hon. Stuart Namm; Peter Neufeld of the Innocence Project, Cardozo Law School; New Yorkers Against the Death Penalty; Jennifer O'Connor of Baker Botts, L.L.P., Washington, D.C.; Terrence C. O'Connor; James F. O'Donnell; Bob Oeser, New York State Division of Parole; Orchid BioSciences, Inc., of Princeton, New Jersey; Arden Ostrander, CBS News Productions; Anthony Papa; Prof. Steven D. Penrod, John Jay College of Criminal Justice; Eleanor Jackson Piel of New York City; John J. Poklemba of Albany; Selwyn Raab; Michael Race, Race Investigations; Michael L. Radelet, University of Colorado; Norman Redlich; Luis Kevin Rojas; Richard Rosen, New York State Division of Criminal Justice Services; Marty Rosenbaum, New York State Senate, Codes Committee; Richard Ross, Division of Criminal Justice Services; Nelson E. Roth, former New York State special prosecutor; Yvette Reyes, Wide World Photos, Associated Press; Barry C. Sample, Office of New York State Comptroller; Ted Schaar, Schaar Communications; Bastienne Schmidt; Eric M. Sears; Tom Seligson, CBS News Productions; Bill Sillery, Division of Criminal Justice Services; Prof. Jerome Skolnick, University of California at Berkeley; Prof. Abbe Smith, Georgetown University Law Center; Marjorie M. Smith of Englander and Smith, Tappan, New York; Nikki Smith, Smith/Skolnik Literary Management; Rex Smith, Albany *Times Union*; Herbert Spiegel, M.D., P.C.; Jed Stone, Chicago attorney; Lawrence F. Spirn of Woodbury, New York; Robert G. Sullivan of Sullivan and Lipakis; Ronald Tabak of Skadden Arps Meagher and Flom, New York City; Martin B. Tankleff; Judith Tannenbaum; Tom Terrizzi, Prisoners Legal Services of New York; Donald Thompson, Rochester attorney; Randolph

F. Treece, Office of the New York State Comptroller; Betty Tyson; Steve Weinberg, Center for Public Integrity; Kelly C. Whitney, Infolution Investigations, Richmond, California; Anthony Ken Umina, former commissioner, New York State Board of Parole; Elaine Utal and Mary Ward, Centurion Ministries; Joe Walsh; Steve Weinberg, Center for Public Interest; Winthrop Wetherbee; Rev. Peter Young; and John Youngblood, New York State Capital Defender Office.

Once again, I value the steady support and sound advice of Eric Zinner, editorial director of New York University Press, and his staff, as well as the input I received from the press's staff and outside reviewers.

Family members and friends who were especially supportive include my parents, Keith and Joyce Christianson; Peter Christianson and Serena Furman; Carol and Tony Archambault, Susie and Jerry Ouellette, Myron and Jetta Gordon, Ralph Blumenthal, Bill Kennedy, Linda Mussmann and Claudia Bruce of Time and Space Ltd.; Alan Raymond, Robert Ruderman and Vicky Sufian, Ken Umina, and Rudy Wurlitzer. I also thank Justin Taylan and Erich W. Schienke, who helped me with images.

As always, I am beholden to my wife, Tamar, for her constant encouragement and guidance, and thankful to my children, Kelly, Emily, and Jonah, for allowing me to keep writing in difficult times.

My guiding principle is this:

Guilt is never to be doubted.

—Franz Kafka, *In the Penal Colony* (1914)

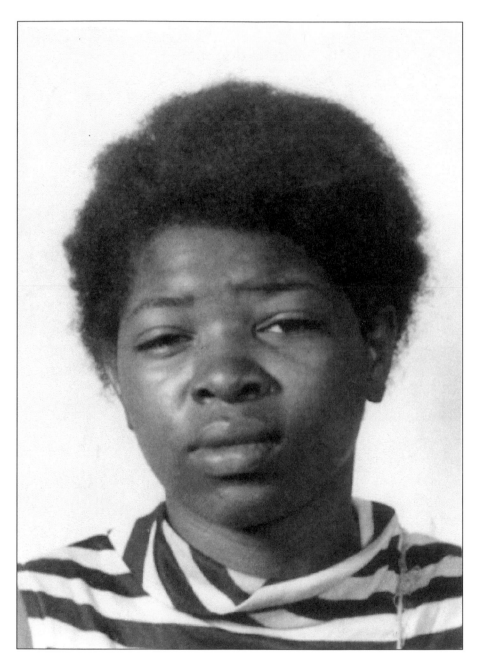

Betty Tyson mugshot. *Courtesy of Rochester Democrat and Chronicle.*

Introduction

Some hard-liners deny that anyone ever gets wrongly convicted. Those in prison, they say, must be guilty of something—otherwise they wouldn't be imprisoned. As they see it, reversals, vacations, or dismissals don't necessarily prove that the defendant was really innocent—just that he somehow "got off." Only the guilty get legally executed; a prisoner freed from death row by DNA demonstrates that "the system works"; the fact that the defendant was erroneously convicted and imprisoned, maybe for years, before an appellate court addressed the problem to them simply represents an inconvenience. Indeed, as far as some naysayers are concerned, the only innocent ones are the unborn. And besides, some assert, the chimera of "innocents" can distract from the overriding problem of what to do about the guilty.

Most rational observers, however, probably recognize that, in addition to its other shortcomings, the criminal justice system produces an unknown number of erroneous determinations of innocence and guilt. Honest mistakes happen. So do dishonest ones. The rich enjoy every kind of protection, but some people are wrongly judged and punished. Usually the defendants adversely affected are poor persons of color. Many members of the public also realize that the criminal justice system tends to circle its wagons. Cops stick together, prosecutors mobilize to ward off any legal challenge, and judges tend to uphold the actions of other judges—tendencies that may make it all the more difficult for the wrongly convicted person to prove his or her innocence.

This book looks inside some actual, specific cases involving individuals who were convicted and imprisoned for crimes they didn't commit—defendants who were innocent although proven guilty—and at the efforts to undo the convictions. A brief graphic rendition is offered for each case. The compilation isn't exhaustive (it probably only scratches the surface), but it reflects a significant problem. Although all the wrongful convictions described herein happened in New York—a state that, in legal matters, is generally considered relatively advanced and sophisticated and often regarded as one of the best—maybe finding such a state of affairs in one of the better places will also raise serious questions about what goes on in the worst. Certainly such problems are not confined to Illinois and Texas—they exist in every state and each jurisdiction.

Most of the cases featured in the book involved a situation where a jury's verdict was overturned and judicial proceedings resulted in what many reasonable observers may construe as an "exoneration," meaning that the defendant was ultimately found blameless. In some of the cases, the State Court of Claims even awarded civil damages pursuant to the Wrongful Conviction and Imprisonment Act of 1984, leaving little doubt that mistakes had resulted in the wrongful imprisonment of an innocent person. In such cases, the defendant's innocence literally had to be and was legally proven. This constitutes an extremely high standard—higher than any prosecutor ever has to meet.

The New York statute requires claimants to establish in pleadings that the conviction was reversed or vacated and that the accusatory instrument was dismissed; or, if a new trial was ordered, either that they were found not guilty or the accusatory instrument was dismissed without a trial. The statute also stipulates that the claimant must establish that the reversal or vacation of the conviction, as well as the dismissal of the accusatory instrument, was made on one or more specific grounds under the Criminal Procedure Law. The act doesn't include all possible grounds consistent with innocence on which a case may be dismissed. It also contains the misleading phrase "in furtherance of justice," which many observers might interpret as being consistent with a proven claim of innocence—yet a claimant whose indictment was dismissed for this reason will not be able to meet the conditions for bringing a claim under the Wrongful Conviction and Imprisonment Act, even if he or she was innocent. Finally, the statute asks claimants to establish in pleadings a substantial likelihood of prevailing at trial; for after a person's conviction has been reversed and the accusatory instrument has been dismissed, the claimant must also prove his or her innocence to the Court of Claims judge by "clear and convincing evidence."

Since the act took effect, fewer than twenty persons have received awards. This includes only a tiny fraction of all wrongful convictions. Unlike other jurisdictions, New York doesn't set an upper limit on the amount it will pay. So far, the biggest individual award has been $1.9 million and the smallest have been $40,000. From January 1, 1985 to June 25, 2001, 165 claims were filed, 131 claims dismissed, 22 claims pending, and 12 awards made. New York is considered the most generous state in compensating wrongful convictions. In thirty-six other states, wrongfully convicted persons are legally barred from recovering damages in a court of law.

Besides including some recently settled matters that have passed muster with the Court of Claims, this book also recalls a few notable wrongful conviction cases from earlier eras as a reminder that the problem isn't new and that a single case (such as *Whitmore*) can sometimes change a whole system.

When this project was started, I selected twelve convicted persons who were still in prison. Not all the convictions in the book were eventually undone, however. At this writing, six have had their convictions reversed and seven of the twelve defendants (Fernando Bermudez, Charles Hamilton, Patsy Kelly Jarrett, Emel McDowell, Rubin Ortega, Frank Sterling, and Martin Tankleff) are still in prison, fighting to be cleared, after serving long terms. Some of them seem almost to have been forgotten by the outside world. But they are excited by the prospect of suddenly winning in court, like others they've read about in the newspapers. Since this book was started, five of the featured subjects who were incarcerated (Lamont Branch, Anthony Faison, Ruben Montalvo, Jose Morales, and Kenneth Pavel) eventually won their freedom, and they were moved to the "exonerated" column. A sixth, Rubin Ortega, was awaiting action by the district attorney. Maybe more movement of this sort will continue to occur over time—but maybe it won't. After all, it's a lot easier to find someone guilty than it is later to prove him innocent;

thus it's likely that some of these convicted-but-not-exonerated persons will never be cleared, never be freed—despite all the evidence in their favor. At any rate, one shouldn't conclude that "the system works." If it did, there wouldn't be any need for this book.

For several decades, a smattering of newspaper stories, books, television pieces, and Hollywood films have focused on the plight of wrongfully convicted persons. Such cries have helped a few prisoners win their freedom. These stories are the rare exception, however, not the rule. More often than not, media outlets represent the world in terms of black and white and good and evil, just as the adversarial system of criminal law clings to Manichaean notions of guilt or innocence, even though the real world is often gray, filled with contradictions, and plagued by doubts. In some instances, sensational, erroneous, or biased news coverage helped lead to the conviction in the first place.

Generally speaking, the news media provide precious little independent or enterprising coverage of criminal cases. If the media follow these cases at all, they tend to dutifully rely on information provided by the police and the courts. Court or legal reporting largely consists of selective trial coverage. Most journalists aren't equipped or inclined to do the tremendous work required to cover a case properly or to scrutinize a criminal conviction, much less to wage the kind of campaign it takes to undo an unjust result. Only a tiny handful of major city newspapers are capable of performing such a role. Even if they inclined to try, alternative newspapers and magazines generally lack the necessary credibility and stature to be effective. Local and even national television news operations rarely initiate such reports. As a result, most areas of the state are left without any likely advocate able to take a second look at a conviction. Yet without investigative reporting by a well-respected news organization, many cases of injustice probably would never result in an amendment—there never would be a reversed conviction or a decision to drop the charges or a finding of liability.

The book's emphasis on journalistic as well as legal aspects reflects the role that publicity plays in the making of a successful wrongful conviction claim, because, quite simply, without strong media support along with their legal assistance, some defendants never would stand a chance.

Fortunately for a few convicted persons, there have been exceptions to the rule—investigative reporters or columnists who pursued the truth and helped correct an injustice. Based on my own first-hand experience as a reporter, I know how difficult it is to prove someone's innocence—even by journalistic standards.

Unfortunately, not much is known about the current nature and extent of wrongful conviction. The state does not maintain a master list of its mistakes. Since Edwin M. Borchard's pathbreaking book *Convicting the Innocent: Sixty-five Actual Errors of Criminal Justice* (1932), a few scholars and writers have sought to document wrongful conviction cases in the United States. Following up on an earlier article published in the *Stanford Law Review* (1987), Radelet and Bedau, writing with Putnam (1996) documented four hundred cases of wrongful conviction, including twenty-three wrongful executions in New York. A study by Huff, Rattner, and Sagarin (1996)—largely based on a survey of criminal justice officials—extrapolated that ten thousand persons per year are wrongfully convicted of serious crimes in the United States. Estimates have ranged as high as 3 to 10 percent of all felony convictions—a staggering number. Yet there is no official database. For a time it seemed that every daily newspaper brought with it mention of another case. But since September 11, 2001, the frequency has drastically decreased. Other problems now seem paramount in the public mind, and "innocence" to some officials has become archaic and quaint—a luxury we can no longer afford.

During the last decade or so, however, the new marvel of deoxyribonucleic acid (DNA) tests positively established, with a high level of scientific certainty, that some convicted persons didn't commit the crime in question. In 1996 the National Institute of Justice of the U.S. Department of Justice issued a report documenting twenty-eight wrongful convictions for murder or sexual assault in fourteen state courts and the District of Columbia wherein postconviction DNA comparison had proven to a scientific certainty that the convicted persons were not guilty.

This powerful scientific tool has suddenly stripped away the armor of infallibility from capital punishment adjudication. As one hundred condemned persons have been freed from death row based on DNA tests and other determinations of wrongful conviction, public support for the death penalty has eroded and prompted at least two governors to establish a moratorium on executions. Yet DNA testing hasn't killed capital punishment, and the parade of errors exposed by DNA hasn't even produced major criminal justice reforms. It may even provide a false sense of security.

This book includes only a few recent episodes where DNA was used or is being sought to help prove a wrongful conviction in New York. As with the vast majority of criminal cases everywhere, DNA seldom enters the picture—whether to convict someone, to rule out a potential suspect, or to free the wrongfully convicted. Unfortunately, DNA can't be counted on to solve most crimes or to overturn the vast majority of wrongful convictions. It isn't a magic bullet or a panacea. And even DNA testing is subject to human error. But it can help to rule out some innocents.

Earlier scholarly studies (by Borchard, Bedau and Radelet, and others) prominently cited several New York death penalty cases among their lists of persons wrongfully executed or almost executed. Rosenbaum (1990–91) cataloged fifty-nine wrongful homicide convictions in New York State from 1965 to 1988. Most of the cases presented in this book were not capital affairs, though a number were murder cases that could have been prosecuted under the state's later death penalty statute or the federal death penalty provisions, both of which were enacted in the 1990s.

It is important to recognize that death penalty cases are not the only instances in which miscarriages of justice have occurred. Several other cases described here involved crimes less serious than murder, and a few convictions came about as a result of a guilty plea rather than a trial verdict.

In fact, wrongful convictions carry serious consequences wherever the deprivation of liberty is at stake. The problem often gets addressed only where very long sentences are involved, because it usually takes several years to gain a reversal, and by then, most criminals are already released. Few legal players pause to consider whether the vast bulk of offenders, who serve two years or so in prison, may include their share of wrongful convictions—even if some of them pleaded guilty. But that is very likely the case.

Under New York's Criminal Procedure Law, a convicted defendant in a noncapital case may challenge his conviction by raising matters outside the trial record, such as newly discovered evidence or ineffective assistance of counsel. This requires the defendant to go back before the same court where the conviction occurred. Judges do not relish such an event. To appeal the judgment in state court, the defendant must take the matter before the Appellate Division (the intermediate state court of appeal). Only after presenting the claims in state court can the defendant then file a habeas corpus challenge in U.S. District Court. But habeas corpus offers slim hope. And clemency offers virtually no hope at all—governors and presidents do not pardon prisoners based on innocence.

Rather than talk about wrongful conviction in global terms, the book tries briefly to examine a number of specific cases in capsule form—a difficult task given the complexities of the events and issues involved. Concise accounts can never do justice to the sufferings endured by so many or convey the hard work put in by all the good police, prosecutors, defense lawyers, investigators, advocates, and judges who struggled to right such wrongs. But they can reveal some common patterns and general characteristics. Collectively, they may provide insight into some of the causes and consequences of wrongful conviction. It is hoped that some of the humanity of those involved will come through.

Most of the material in the book was gleaned from legal case files—briefs, smoking-gun memoranda, investigative reports, police videotapes, judicial opinions, and the like—that were shared by defense attorneys, defendants, and court officials. The New York Police Department was unwilling to provide arrest mug shot photographs, so other images had to be compiled. Data were also obtained from interviews conducted in 2001 and early 2002 with more than two hundred persons. Additional information was gathered from books and articles that appeared in newspapers, magazines, and journals. All this has been filtered through my own professional experience in the criminal justice system, which goes back more than thirty years. I am not a lawyer, but my Ph.D. in criminal justice and work in the trenches has entailed gaining familiarity with the criminal justice process.

The stories are grouped according to the some of the variables that are generally recognized as major contributing factors to wrongful convictions—factors such as presumed guilt, mistaken identification, ineffective counsel, eyewitness perjury, false confessions, police misconduct, prosecutorial misconduct, fabrication of evidence, and forensics. However, these categories are both artificial and neither all-inclusive nor exclusive. Other reasons contribute to miscarriages of justice. By all accounts, most wrongful convictions involve more than one underlying cause, and some involve many factors.

In most cases, it wouldn't be fair to point the finger solely at a single culprit—that is, police, prosecutors, defense attorneys, trial judges, juries, appellate courts, or legislators. Wrongful conviction is a team sport. But that shouldn't absolve everyone from responsibility. As it stands, the responsible parties are seldom held accountable—voted out of office, dismissed, disciplined, or subject to civil damages. Most often, they never even acknowledge their mistakes, much less apologize for them. No official inquiry gets to the bottom of the matter; no public report sets forth the reasons for the errors; and no successful legislation corrects the chronic underlying causes. Consequently, some errors persist and are repeated. North Carolina has created an independent commission to review how innocent people get convicted and what can be done to address wrongful conviction, but New York has ducked the issue.

One of the most overlooked aspects of the problem is that cases of wrongful conviction represent instances where the real criminals go unpunished. More often than not, freeing the "wrong man" does nothing to help bring the guilty party to justice. This fact often gets swept under the rug. Sometimes the same mistaken prosecutor already has awarded the real killer immunity from prosecution or allowed the statute of limitations to pass. As a result, the crime victim may again feel cheated, abandoned, or ashamed.

In a few instances, persons who were found to have been wrongfully convicted have later gone on to be rightly convicted for other crimes, which raises other questions. The fact that someone was the victim of a miscarriage of justice does not necessarily mean they are a good and noble person. But some of them are.

A wrongful conviction case serves as a microcosm of what goes on every day in the administration of justice. Often the errors are simply not caught. But sometimes a case can prove a Pandora's box, exposing all sorts of deep-seated problems, widespread corruptions, inexcusable practices, and systemic abuses. No wonder officials try to clamp a lid on such cases before a whole office or department becomes implicated. Without such damage control, one can only wonder how many other cases might disintegrate or explode.

At the same time, most wrongful conviction cases represent a personal and professional triumph, because undoing a felony conviction represents a tremendous feat. More often than not, it could not be achieved without close collaboration involving many people, some of them strangers and often at least one of them an "angel." Thus every story entails terrible misfortune but also great perseverance. Sometimes there is also vindication and redemption, for such a case can bring out the best as well as the worst.

Above all, wrongful convictions represent tragic and costly flaws in our system of justice, our society. Often these actions go largely undetected or unnoticed, except by the actual criminals and their hidden victims—the wrongly convicted. But they are not invisible, insignificant, or nonexistent. As Martin Luther King Jr. said, "Injustice anywhere is a threat to justice everywhere." And punishment of the innocent makes a mockery of the law.

The New York State Court of Appeals. *Author's photo.*

SUPREME COURT OF THE STATE OF NEW YORK
COUNTY OF NEW YORK   Indictment # 8759/91
PEOPLE OF THE STATE OF NEW YORK

                         Respondent

         -against-

FERNANDO BERMUDEZ
                         Defendant
_____

SUPREME COURT OF THE STATE OF NEW YORK)
) ss:
COUNTY OF NEW YORK   )

I, Leonard J. Macaluso, residing at ▓▓▓▓▓▓▓▓▓▓▓, NY 10034,
being duly sworn, depose and say:

On April 2, 1993 I told Mary Ann Di Bari, Esq., the following
about my video-taped and written statements to Detective Massanova
and Assistant District Attorney James Rodriguez, conducted a few
hours after Fernando Bermudez was arrested on August 6, 1991:

During the course of interviews, I informed Mr. Rodriguez and
Detective Massanova that I was with Fernando Bermudez from
approximately twelve (12 P.M.) noon on Saturday August 3, 1991
until Approximately five fifteen (5:15 A.M.) on Sunday, August 4,
1991; and that during these hours Fernando Bermudez left me only to
use the urinal in the men's lavatory for a few minutes. During the
course of interviews I also attested to the following facts:

> Fernando Bermudez and I, along with friends, were taking turns
> enjoying and driving a green 1990 BMW, [which had been
> purchased by Mr. Bermudez Sr., after it was crashed and sold
> "as is" for $3000.00 at an auction]. We had just picked up
> the car after waiting [five months] for it to be repaired and
> rebuilt, and that Saturday, August 3, 1991 was a special,
> long-anticipated day -- a day to get and drive and enjoy the
> car! We did enjoy the car -- spent most of our time in the
> car listening to music, driving and flirting a little. We

paused briefly to observe the night life in Manhattan and to eat a big meal at the BBQ a restaurant noted for great food, huge portions and cheap prices. We **At No Time** went to the Marc Ballroom; fought with anyone, or committed any act violent or criminal in nature. On the contrary, [I stated then and I do repeat now], we did nothing more than enjoy each other's company and the exhilaration of experiencing the feel of the newly-acquired car.

My statements also included a description of the clothing Fernando was wearing August 3-4, 1991, which consisted of blue jeans and a Banana Republic T-shirt with small Roman letters on the hem of the pocket. I stated in addition, that Fernando was clean shaven and had no facial hair except for a slight moustache.

I am certain of these facts and the fact that Fernando Bermudez is innocent. I have never committed a crime. I neither smoke nor drink. I have an Associates degree in electronics and computers and am presently employed at Columbia University: Inward Community Services, where I was employed at the time of my taped interview.

Moreover, I have expressed my willingness and eagerness to take a polygraph test so as to further the interests of truth and justice in this matter.

Leonard J. Macaluso

Sworn to before me on
April/6, 1993
Mary Ann Di Bari, Esq.
Notary Public; State of New York
County of Westchester
Notary No. 4997226
Commission expires 06/01/94

MARY ANN DI BARI, ESQ.
Notary Public, State of New York
No. 60 4997226
Qualified in Westchester County
Commission Expires June 1, 1994

II

SUPREME COURT OF THE STATE OF NEW YORK
COUNTY OF NEW YORK
FERNANDO BERMUDEZ
                    Movant,

          -against-   Indictment No. 8759/91

PEOPLE OF THE STATE OF NEW YORK
                                             AFFIDAVIT
                    Respondent,

STATE OF NEW YORK   )
) ss:
COUNTY OF NEW YORK   )

          Deponent, _EFRAIN LOPEZ_, being duly sworn/ affirms
under penalty of perjury the following:

I am of legal age, residing at _RIKERS ISLAND_

and I have personal knowledge of certain facts relating to the
above-captioned case:

AS I stated in my Affidavit of
September 1992. I was threatened by
Detective Massanova in this case, and
told that if I did not identify
Fernando Bermudez, as the shooter, of Raymond Blout
and Detective MASSANOVA Pointed to (E.L.)
that I would be charged as the shooter,
the photo of Fernando Bermudez, Saying
he was a drug dealer and that he
was the shooter. In point fact, I did
not see Bermudez in the Marc ball room
on august 3 and 4th, "1991" I have NEVER
seen him before in my life.

12

and he is not "wool lou", as I stated
in my video statement to the police. In
fact, I know who the real killer is) I was
in fear of my life. and coerced into
indentifying Bermudez, "wool lou" in fact is
Luis Munoz and "wool lou" is the shooter.
on August 6, 1993 in the presence of
Mary Ann Di Bari and Ⓔ Ⓛ adele Janow I
look At 21 color pictures. I SAW Ⓔ Ⓛ LUIS
MUNOZ in one of the photo's "photo # Ⓔ Ⓛ" Exhibit F
I Reconized A few of my friends but I
did'nt SEE them do anything wrong. Ⓔ Ⓛ Nobody
threatened me of promised me anything. I
Just want to SEE the truth and JUSTICE,

Sworn to before me this
6 day of August, 1993

Efrain Lopez
_____
EFRAIN LOPEZ

Mary Ann Di Bar
Mary Ann Di Bari, Esq.
Notary Public No. 60-4997226;
State of New York
Commission expires June 1, 1994

Adele L. Janow

13

Even a modestly competent district attorney

can get a grand jury to indict a ham sandwich.

—New York Chief Judge Sol Wachtler

A Brooklyn grand jury at lunch in 1951. *Courtesy of Life magazine*

I

Presumed Guilty

Voltaire said, "It is better to risk saving a guilty person than to condemn an innocent one"; and Blackstone wrote, "It is better that ten guilty persons escape than one innocent suffer." Many Americans naturally assume that accused persons are considered innocent until proven guilty, that our adversarial legal system protects the innocent, and that any rare miscarriages of justice brought to light will ultimately be corrected. In fact, however, the presumption of innocence isn't guaranteed by the Constitution of the United States. At least, that is what the Supreme Court concluded in *Herrera v. Collins* (1993), when it found that a claim of actual innocence is not itself a constitutional claim. The majority opinion in that decision, written by Chief Justice William Rehnquist, held that innocence is not the concern of the federal courts—a person convicted in state court can bring a claim in federal court that the trial had been unfair in its procedures, but not in its results.

According to a leading expert on habeas corpus, Professor Eric M. Freedman of Hofstra Law School, "It has never happened at the United States Supreme Court level that someone has been released on federal habeas grounds that he or she is innocent of the crime." The Rehnquist

Court didn't find anything wrong when Congress eviscerated habeas corpus, thereby greatly reducing prisoners' ability to gain access to the federal courts for legal redress. And the states, including New York, have not done better than the federal government at safeguarding the presumption of innocence. As a result of such thinking and the stronger presumption of guilt that has arisen in executive, legislative, and judicial quarters, the incidence of wrongful convictions has likely actually increased, not diminished, in recent years, particularly as funding for the defense has failed to keep pace with funding for law enforcement and prosecution.

Innocence is often considered irrelevant in war, and this can hold true whether the campaign is waged on crime, drugs, terrorism, or a foreign power. As happens in other forms of combat, some innocent bystanders end up becoming "collateral damage"—in this instance, wrongfully convicted. This dynamic was forcefully demonstrated in the midst of this study, in relation to September 11 and its immediate aftermath. Suddenly, innocence seemed to have become expendable in some areas of the American legal system.

In reality, however, the presumption of innocence had been under assault for some time. More than thirty years ago, the late Herbert L. Packer and other legal scholars asserted that the criminal justice system doesn't operate to clear "innocent" suspects—it tries to bring the "guilty" to justice. Some of them pointed out that, at least from the point of arrest and increasingly throughout the rest of the criminal justice process, the system generally operates on a presumption of guilt. In practical terms, that is what enables the machinery to handle such large numbers of cases. Without it, and its attendant practices such as offender profiling, plea-bargaining and pretrial detention, the criminal justice apparatus probably wouldn't function as smoothly as it does—it might get overwhelmed, like Kafka's harrow in "In the Penal Colony."

And so, once the police have made their arrest, based on "probable cause" that the person committed a crime, prosecutors generally tend to presume that the accused is probably guilty of something. So do most juries. As then Chief Justice Sol Wachtler put it, "Even a modestly competent district attorney can get a grand jury to indict a ham sandwich."

But as former judge Wachtler himself later came to better appreciate after his own arrest, the tilt toward guilt doesn't end at indictment.

Once someone is indicted for a felony, the chances are incredibly high that he or she will be convicted. In 2000, for instance, New York's conviction rate from felony indictments disposed stood at a whopping 100 percent in four counties, 98 percent or higher in nine others, and over 90 percent for the state as a whole. This tendency indicates a greater potential for wrongful conviction.

Much of the high conviction percentage is a function of admissions of guilt. In New York, as in most other states, the overwhelming proportion of felony convictions are obtained by guilty pleas, not trials. In 2000, for example, 95.7 percent of New York's convictions arose from pleas; for drug cases, 97.3 percent were convicted by guilty plea; and for violent felony offenses, 89.9 percent were convicted by plea.

In such cases, the defendant admits guilt and agrees to the likely sentence before it is imposed—not the sort of scenario, one might think, that would produce many wrongful convictions (especially since those who plead guilty may forfeit their right of appeal). Yet plea-bargaining is notoriously coercive and dishonest—so much so that one of the leading scholarly experts, Professor John Langbein of the University of Chicago Law School, has compared the practice to "ancient medieval torture," the modern equivalent of confession. And like torture, instead of getting at the truth, plea-bargaining may simply pressure some defendants to cop a plea to cut their losses. Prosecutors and judges have become so dependent on plea-bargaining that they end up trying to penalize anyone who exercises his or her right to trial. Prosecutors manage to achieve their sky-high conviction rates largely by forcing a high percentage of defendants to admit to a lesser offense. Overburdened public defenders and assigned counsel encourage their clients to plead guilty in order to avoid having to spend scarce time and resources on a single case. Defendants plead guilty to avoid harsher punishment. And judges preside over the negotiated justice process to avoid becoming overwhelmed with impossible backlogs.

In many instances, plea-bargaining serves everyone's interests. But when the defendant is innocent, it can lead to injustice, such as occurred in Queens in 1993 in the case of sixteen-year-old Lambert Charles. After a witness identified him in a police lineup as the person who had shot someone to death, the youth confessed to the crime, and on the advice of his Legal Aid attorney he pleaded guilty to first-degree manslaughter. Years later the district attorney agreed to reinvestigate the case and determined that Charles was innocent. Supreme Court Justice Robert J. Hanophy set aside the conviction.

Reversals in plea-bargained cases are highly unusual, however. With rare exceptions, once someone is convicted, by plea or trial, the die is cast. From that point, the law maintains a strong presumption of guilt.

This is also true in practical, operational, bureaucratic, and political terms. Prosecutors, for instance, do not like to admit making mistakes. In the 1930s, a prosecuting attorney assured Edwin Borchard, "Innocent men are never convicted. Don't worry about it, it never happens in the world. It is a physical impossibility." This kind of comment is still made today. A prosecutorial advocate stated as much to me during an interview for this book. There are instances, of course, where district attorneys (DAs) have gone on record as saying that innocent persons should never be held in prison, and other such comforting things; but these instances are rare, and the DAs' assistants are not empowered or inclined to make such statements on their own account.

Judges can also contribute to the problem. Some trial judges consistently make rulings that favor the prosecution above the law. Appellate courts also tend to uphold convictions. Judge Learned Hand, a staunchly conservative jurist, famously proclaimed long ago, in *United States v. Garsson*, 291 F. 646, 649 (S.D.N.Y. 1923), "Our procedure has always been haunted by the ghost of the innocent man convicted. It is an unreal dream. What we need to fear is the archaic formalism and the watery sentiment that obstruct, delays, and defeats the prosecution of crime." Such judicial attitudes haven't changed for the better over the years, particularly as more and more judges have been selected from the ranks of former prosecutors.

Such attitudes can also be present among criminal defense lawyers—and not only among overburdened and underpaid court-appointed counsel or public defenders. One noted and high-priced trial attorney told me, "I don't believe I've ever had an innocent defendant who was convicted. Some guilty ones who got acquitted maybe, but not an innocent client railroaded into prison."

Still, mistakes have happened, and although mistakes in capital cases can prove fatal, erroneous convictions have occurred there as well. Some early historical studies showed a higher incidence of wrongful convictions in New York capital cases than anywhere else. Writing in 1965, the New York State Temporary Commission on Revision of the Penal Law and Criminal Code—a bipartisan legislative panel—concluded, "Some erroneous convictions are inevitable in the course of the enforcement of the penal law and error sometimes cannot be established until time has passed. Such errors cannot be corrected after execution. An injustice of this kind destroys the moral force of the entire penal law." The danger of wrongful convictions was an important reason that the panel recommended (and the state imposed) a moratorium on legal executions that lasted for decades.

Some legal scholars, such as Professor Samuel R. Gross of the University of Michigan Law School, contend that wrongful convictions may actually be more prevalent in death penalty cases. They theorize that the most heinous crimes may put added pressure on prosecutors to win a conviction, and the requirements of the capital punishment legal system may also weed out jurors who might be inclined toward the defense. But others contend that the opposite may be true—that because capital cases entail greater scrutiny and more adversarial proceedings, they may be less susceptible to error than noncapital cases. Capital cases in states using the death penalty do show a higher rate of reversal than other cases where less serious penalties are involved. Yet this might be because it is unfeasible for lesser offenders to contest their conviction.

Innocent defendants can end up being penalized at a number of key decision points. In exchange for fully cooperating with the police, a person may make himself more likely to be arrested. For refusing to plead guilty and insisting on a trial, an innocent defendant may risk a stiffer sentence if convicted. By continuing to assert his innocence in prison and trying to set himself apart from criminals, a prisoner may incur the wrath of other inmates. Believing that he has not committed an offense, he may refuse to participate in counseling or other rehabilitation programs that could speed his release. Appearing before the parole board, he may not show remorse, thereby lessening his chances of getting let out of prison.

Burden of Proof

The New York State Office of Court Administration has offered the following guidance for jury members:

> The defendant is not required to prove that he/she is not guilty. In fact, the defendant is not required to prove anything. To the contrary, the People have the burden of proving the defendant guilty beyond a reasonable doubt. That means, before you can find the defendant guilty of a crime, the People must prove beyond a reasonable doubt every element of the crime and that the defendant is the person who committed that crime. The burden of proof never shifts from the People to the defendant. If the People fail to satisfy their burden of proof, you must find the defendant not guilty.
>
> What does our law mean when it requires proof of guilt "beyond a reasonable doubt"?
>
> The law uses the term, "proof beyond a reasonable doubt," to tell you how strong the evidence of guilt must be to permit a verdict of guilty. The law recognizes that, in dealing with human affairs, there are very few things in this world that we know with absolute certainty. Therefore, the law does not require the People to prove a defendant guilty beyond all possible doubt. On the other hand, it is not sufficient to prove that the defendant is probably guilty. In a criminal case, the proof of guilt must be stronger than that. It must be beyond a reasonable doubt.
>
> Proof beyond a reasonable doubt is proof that leaves you so firmly convinced of the defendant's guilt that you have no reasonable doubt of the existence of any element of the crime or of the defendant's identity as the person who committed the crime.
>
> A reasonable doubt is an honest doubt of the defendant's guilt for which a reason exists based upon the nature and quality of the evidence. The doubt can arise from the evidence that was presented or from the lack of material and convincing evidence.
>
> A reasonable doubt is not a fanciful or imaginary doubt. It is a doubt that a reasonable person, acting in a matter of this importance, would be likely to entertain because of the evidence or because of the lack of material and convincing evidence.

In determining whether or not the People have proven the defendant's guilt beyond a reasonable doubt, you should be guided solely by a full and fair evaluation of the evidence. Your verdict must not rest upon outlandish theories or baseless speculations. Nor may your verdict be influenced in any way by bias, prejudice, sympathy, or a desire to bring an end to your deliberations or to avoid an unpleasant duty.

After you have carefully evaluated the evidence, determine which evidence you accept, and then decide whether that evidence convinces you beyond a reasonable doubt of the defendant's guilt. If you are not convinced beyond a reasonable doubt that the defendant is guilty of the crime, you must find the defendant not guilty of that crime. If you are convinced beyond a reasonable doubt that the defendant is guilty of a charged crime, you must find the defendant guilty of that crime.

—From the New York State Office of Court Administration,
Committee on Criminal Jury Instructions (Albany, 2000)

Charge to the Jury

The Criminal Procedure Law 300.10(1)(2) provides:

1. At the conclusion of the summations, the court must deliver a charge to the jury.

2. In its charge, the court must state the fundamental legal principles applicable to criminal cases in general. Such principles include, but are not limited to, the presumption of the defendant's innocence, the requirement that guilt be proved beyond a reasonable doubt and that the jury may not in determining the issue of guilt or innocence, consider or speculate concerning matters relating to sentence or punishment. Upon request of a defendant who did not testify in his own behalf, but not otherwise, the court must state that the fact that he did not testify is not a factor from which any inference unfavorable to the defendant may be drawn. The court must also state the material legal principles applicable to the particular case, and, so far as practicable, explain the application of the law to the facts, but it need not marshal or refer to the evidence to any greater extent than is necessary for such explanation.

Overturning a Conviction

The most common legal route for a convicted person to overturn a conviction involves going back to the trial court to submit a 440 motion under the following state law.

Criminal Procedure Law

ARTICLE 440.10. Motion to vacate judgment.

At any time after entry of a judgment, the court in which it was entered may, upon motion of the defendant, vacate such judgment upon the ground that:

> The court did not have jurisdiction of the action or of the person of the defendant; or
>
> The judgment was procured by duress, misrepresentation or fraud on the part of the court or a prosecutor or a person acting for or in behalf of a court or a prosecutor; or
>
> Material evidence adduced at a trial resulting in the judgment was false and was, prior to the entry of the judgment, known by the prosecutor or by the court to be false; or
>
> Material evidence adduced by the people at a trial resulting in the judgment was procured in violation of the defendant's rights under the constitution of this state or of the United States; or
>
> During the proceedings resulting in the judgment, the defendant, by reason of mental disease or defect, was incapable of understanding or participating in such proceedings; or
>
> Improper and prejudicial conduct not appearing in the record occurred during a trial resulting in the judgment which conduct, if it had appeared in the record, would have required a reversal of the judgment upon an appeal therefrom; or
>
> New evidence has been discovered since the entry of a judgment which could not have been produced by the defendant at trial even with the due diligence on his part and which is of such character as to create the probability that had such evidence been received at the trial the verdict would have been more favorable to the defendant; provided that a motion

based upon such ground must be made with due diligence after the discovery of such alleged new evidence; or

The judgment was obtained in violation of a right of the defendant under the constitution of this state or of the United States.

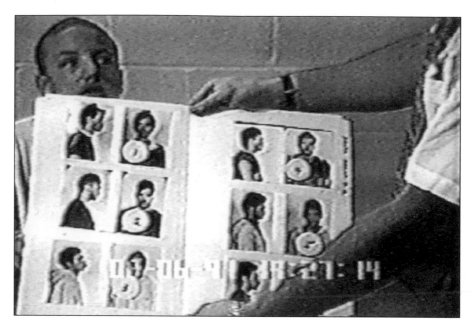

Bermudez photo array.

2

Mistaken Identification

For more than seventy years, studies of wrongful conviction have ascribed one of the leading causes to mistaken witness identification. In his pioneering outline of sixty-five instances where the person convicted was "completely innocent" of the crime, Borchard (1932) found it to be a contributing factor in more than half the cases. Based on a national survey of judges, prosecutors, public defenders, sheriffs, and police, C. Ronald Huff, Arye Rattner, and Edward Sagarin (1996) found that mistaken identification figured in more than 52 percent of the wrongful convictions. Barry Scheck, Peter Neufeld, and Jim Dwyer (2000), included mistaken identification as a known factor in 81 percent of seventy-four wrongful conviction cases that later resulted in an exoneration from DNA.

Eyewitness identification has long been known to be extremely unreliable. On reviewing the evidence in *The Case of Sacco and Vanzetti,* Felix Frankfurter (1927: 30) asked, "What is the worth of identification testimony even when uncontradicted? The identification of strangers is proverbially untrustworthy. The hazards of such testimony are established by a formidable number of instances in the records of English and

American trials. These instances are recent—not due to the brutalities of ancient criminal procedure."

Forty years later, in *United States v. Wade* (1967), the U.S. Supreme Court concluded that "the annals of criminal law are rife with instances of mistaken identification." The question is, how do they occur and what can be done to prevent their occurrence? To minimize the potential for error, the Court issued a series of decisions—*Wade, Gilbert v. California* (1967), and *Stovall v. Denno* (1967)—mandating various procedures governing police lineups and other identification techniques. Additional rulings over the years have sought to establish tighter requirements for other means of eyewitness identification. But these limits are often tested.

Mistaken eyewitnesses are often highly convincing because they are so sincere and persuasive, even though they are wrong. Witnesses can be very susceptible to suggestions or pressure by the police. And their recollections may tend to discriminate against members of other racial groups. As a result, some eyewitness testimony is not reliable.

A person who is mistakenly identified by a crime victim or a witness cannot recover civil damages from either, unless it can be shown that the prosecution was baseless and the complaint was made with malice.

Yet eyewitness accounts continue to provide the foundation, and sometimes the only basis, for many prosecutions. And errors continue to be made.

Queens

Hitchcock's *The Wrong Man*

After reading articles in *Life* magazine and *Reader's Digest* in 1953, and watching a dramatic version that appeared on national television, movie director Alfred Hitchcock began making a movie about the nightmare experience of Christopher (Manny) Balestrero, a bass player at Manhattan's ritzy Stork Club, who had been arrested and jailed for a series of armed robberies he didn't commit—because he'd been mistakenly identified as the culprit.

Filmed on location where it happened in Queens, Hitchcock's *noir* version featured an Everyman character (played by Henry Fonda) who suddenly finds himself hauled one night into the police station. A lieutenant tells him, "An innocent man has nothing to fear, remember that Manny," then snaps on the cuffs. Balestrero remains accused until a shopkeeper later catches his "double" during another robbery attempt—but only after the innocent man has been forced to endure tremendous fear and humiliation, and his wife has suffered a nervous breakdown. And Balestrero had only been arrested, not convicted.

Balestrero's defense lawyer, Frank O'Connor, was depicted as a major character in the film, and he later became district attorney of Queens County (1956–66), president of the New York State District Attorneys Association, a state senator, president of the New York City Council, the Democratic candidate for governor against Nelson Rockefeller (1966), and state supreme court judge.

Henry Fonda (*left*) as Manny Balestro and Richard Robbins as the real culprit in Alfred Hitchcock's movie *The Wrong Man* (1957). *Couresy of Floyd McCarty, MPTV.net*

Throughout his distinguished career, O'Connor championed more scientific procedures to protect innocent persons from wrongful arrest and conviction and opposed both capital punishment and life without parole. As a justice on the Appellate Division, he wrote a landmark state opinion establishing better guidelines for eyewitness identification.

Police escort Rojas to squad car for a "show-up" before assembled witnesses.
Courtesy of Priscilla Chenoweth.

New York

People v. Luis Rojas

Luis Kevin Rojas was a popular eighteen-year-old New Jersey high school graduate who was planning to study photography in college. The son of hard-working Colombian immigrants, he had no criminal record and a good reputation.

At 2 A.M. on November 18, 1990, he and a friend were on a subway train in Manhattan, waiting for it to pull out of the Ninth Street Station, after a night on the town. Suddenly, another Hispanic youth they didn't know burst into the car with police officers and pointed at Rojas. The stranger said Rojas was wearing a bright orange jacket—just like the guy he said had shot his friend.

The cops took Rojas and another youth to a crime scene in Greenwich Village and placed them in a squad car in front of a crowd of distraught teenagers. The Hispanic man from the subway car also arrived, and in front of the others he kept accusing Rojas and the other youth as the attackers. In the course of this police "show-up," some of the other teenagers not surprisingly also identified Rojas as an attacker.

Rojas and the other youth were held on charges ranging from attempted murder and weapon possession to riot and coercion. When one of the injured teens died, Rojas was formally charged with murder.

The Manhattan district attorney's office offered him a four-year prison sentence for unlawful possession of a weapon, in exchange for a guilty plea. But Rojas refused, saying he was innocent. A judge dismissed charges against the other defendant, but Rojas remained in custody.

To defend him, his family hired a friendly private attorney, without knowing that he lacked relevant experience.

Rojas in prison.
Courtesy of Priscilla Chenoweth.

Rojas's diabetic mother cried softly from her wheelchair as the judge instructed the jury. She told a reporter, "I believe that he's innocent and that he's going to come home." But after deliberating for fourteen hours, the panel found Luis Kevin Rojas guilty of murder in the second degree, criminal facilitation, first-degree assault, and weapons charges. On February 26, 1992, he was sentenced to fifteen years to life.

Priscilla Chenoweth (right) and Lesley Chenoweth Estevao. *Author's photo.*

A New Jersey woman, Lesley Chenoweth Estevao, read about the case in her local newspaper and told her mother about it. (Everyone who knew Rojas insisted he would never do such a thing.) The mother, Priscilla Read Chenoweth, was a sixty-two-year-old widow of modest means who lived in Kearney, New Jersey, and worked as senior case digest editor for the *New Jersey Law Journal.* She had a law degree but hadn't practiced since 1974.

Chenoweth started looking into the matter. The more she learned, the more she was shocked by the flimsy evidence, poor defense, shoddy police work, abusive prosecution, and official arrogance that marked the case. After visiting Rojas in prison, she became convinced he was innocent.

With her daughter's help, Chenoweth went to work building a proper defense, dipping into her retirement savings to pay for it. By the time she was through, she had spent over $50,000 of her own money, risked her health, and dedicated years of hard work and personal sacrifice to prove her point.

Chenoweth's chief adversary, Manhattan district attorney Robert M. Morgenthau, had been for many years (and still is) New York's most powerful law enforcement official—not someone to trifle with. The assistant district attorney handling the case, Peter Kougasian, was a fifteen-year veteran of Morgenthau's elite staff who was also an accomplished professional nightclub magician. And Kougasian continued to insist that Rojas was guilty.

As Kougasian and Chenoweth parried back and forth, Rojas served more than four and a half years in prison and suffered the death of his mother.

But when it came time to file their appeal, the defense enjoyed some good fortune. One of those submitting an *amicus* brief was former U.S. district judge Harold R. Tyler—one of the city's most highly respected legal figures. In July 1995 the Appellate Division, First Department, unanimously reversed the conviction, vacated the sentence, suppressed the on-scene show-up and lineup identifications, and remanded the case back to supreme court in Manhattan for another trial "if warranted." In their opinion, the justices cited Rojas's original lawyer's "poor preparation, ignorance of the facts and ineffective performance." Chenoweth was elated.

Rojas was freed on bail, but Morgenthau's office stubbornly would not drop the charges and forced him to undergo another trial. Ultimately, however, with unflagging support from Chenoweth and her daughter, dogged work by a private eye, and *pro bono* lawyering by top criminal defender Jethro M. Eisenstein, he was acquitted and freed. He sued for damages under the Wrongful Conviction and Imprisonment Act.

In 2002 his lawyers won an out-of-court settlement of $850,000 from the state, and Rojas gave Chenoweth her money back.

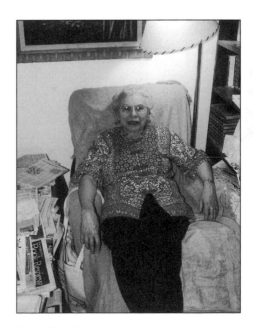

Priscilla Chenoweth, resting.
Author's photo.

Kings

"I'm Going to Turn You Out"

Robert (Bobby) McLaughlin was convicted of robbery and murder in Kings County in 1981 and sentenced to fifteen years to life. But McLaughlin's foster father, Harold Hohne, always believed in his son's innocence and started his own investigation.

A new lawyer, famed civil rights attorney Richard Emery, finally convinced the DA to reopen the case. Brooklyn district attorney Elizabeth Holtzman took the extraordinary step of recommending to Governor Mario Cuomo that McLaughlin's sentence be commuted, claiming that "further incarceration would be unfair." But Cuomo declined her invitation.

In 1986, Supreme Court Justice Ann Feldman set aside the conviction, and the indictment was dismissed. McLaughlin was released after serving six years on his wrongful conviction. After being let out, he said, "If there was a death penalty in this state I would now be ashes in an urn on my mom's mantel."

In 1989, Judge Adolph C. Orlando of the Court of Claims issued his decision in McLaughlin's suit against the state. He found that McLaughlin had never made any incriminatory statement, and two witnesses had confirmed that he was elsewhere at the time of the crime. Identification procedures used by the police were erroneous, improperly suggestive, and constitutionally impermissible. McLaughlin's truthfulness has been established by lie detector tests, whereas the chief witness against him was found to be unreliable. Orlando's review of the case also summarized some of the hardships that McLaughlin had endured as a result of his wrongful conviction.

> He entered the penal system as a slight, rather hard-to-handle, 150-pound, 20 year old, and was released as a 199-pound battle-scarred veteran, attempting to cope with freedom unfamiliar to him for so long. . . .
>
> On entering the prison population at these different facilities, statements like "check out that ass," "we're going to have you when you get out of that cell," "we're going to fuck you in the ass," "I'm going to make

Bobby McLaughlin and his lawyer Richard Emery. *Courtesy of Richard Emery.*

you my girl," "I'm going to turn you out," placed him in constant fear of being raped, assaulted and killed.

Although there is no evidence that he was in fact physically abused, the constant stress, generated by the threat of physical abuse, ultimately led to various physical ailments, i.e., he contracted tuberculosis, he developed migraine headaches from which he still suffers to date, and heart palpitations.

Claimant described in detail how he was always fearful of being the subject of all kinds of violence. To avoid being turned into a "punk" (a slave for the "daddy" who would command all kinds of favors, including sexual deviation), one had to be constantly prepared to fight. Indeed, he testified it was much safer to be locked in a cell than to wander about the facility, or remain in an unlocked cell.

Claimant was also exposed to events that at the very least threatened his safety, and indeed, his life. At one point, he was caught in the middle of a riot. At another time, an inmate was stabbed in the back two feet from him. As a consequence, he was constantly looking over his shoulder, aware that as a "cracker" (white male) he was always a prime target.

At trial, the claimant produced two expert witnesses. . . . Both experts concluded that claimant was suffering from "PTSD" (post-traumatic stress disorder), and that the symptoms stemmed from or were exacerbated by the effects of the long incarceration. The experts also opined that the emotional numbing and the feeling of worthlessness, resulting from the long incarceration and stress, taken together would in all likelihood persist for a period of many years. They testified that the constant reliving of the violence experienced within the prison environment all form a part of this man's psyche, which will perhaps remain with him forever. It is an experience clearly out of the ordinary course of a normal existence.

McLaughlin received an award of $1,940,805—the highest amount granted thus far to a single person under the Court of Claims law. His story was turned into a TV movie titled *Guilty until Proven Innocent* (TVM, 1991), starring Brendan Fraser and Martin Sheen.

Kings

A Suggestive Show-up Procedure

Andre Jackson was convicted of murder and possession of a weapon in Kings County in 1987 and sentenced to fifteen years to life. The conviction was later thrown out.

As his lawyer later successfully argued, he'd been convicted because "the police utilized a suggestive show-up procedure rather than a proper line-up. . . . Obviously, with a fair line-up, the procedure consciously avoided by the police, not even a semi-identification would have been made; Mr. Jackson would have been released; and an innocent man would not have spent over four years in prison."

In December 1991, Jackson's claim for $50 million resulted in an award of $302,100 by Judge S. Michael Nadel of the Court of Claims.

Kings

How Can One Compensate?

Gregory Reed was convicted of murder in Kings County in 1979 and sentenced to fifteen years to life. The Court of Appeals overturned the conviction in 1985 on the grounds that the testimony of the sole witness contained important contradictions, and the indictment was dismissed. He was released after serving six and a half years.

In 1989, Reed was awarded $495,000 by the Court of Claims for his unjust conviction and imprisonment. Judge Adolph C. Orlando wrote in his decision:

> It is always difficult to compensate someone for injuries he or she may have sustained. It is doubly difficult when the Court is asked to determine the loss of someone's freedom. How does one place a price on a fundamental birthright? How can this Court place itself within the experience of the claimant? How does one feel when handcuffed and shackled and placed in a cell as above described? How can a monetary value be placed on the fleeting hope for freedom; the despair that sets in as the iron bars shut behind one? The unmistakable, unforgettable sound that reverberates throughout one's very bones (cf. *Hoffner v. State of New York*, 207 Misc 1070). How can one replace the emotional contact of loved ones forever gone?
>
> No one can really understand the loss of freedom, liberty so unjustly taken from another, "COMPRENDERE NON LO PUO CHI NON LO PROVA."
>
> In spite of the tremendous burden placed upon it, this Court must find damages based on all the evidence before it, keeping in mind that liberty is absolute and the loss of it, the greatest of all human injustices.

Queens County Courthouse. *Author's photo.*

Queens

A Pair of Boots

On a hot June night in 1994, Lee Anthony Long was about to celebrate his thirty-fourth birthday when two plainclothes police officers cuffed him behind his back and took him to an ambulance where a woman he didn't know accused him of assaulting and robbing her at knifepoint in a Queens parking lot. "That's him," she told police.

The woman hadn't seen her assailant's face, or Long's. But she said she recognized him by his boots, even though she said she'd only felt them and not seen them during the attack. Despite the lack of evidence, and although he had a good alibi for his whereabouts at the time of the crime, Lee Long was arrested; tried; convicted of rape, sexual abuse, and robbery; and sentenced to eight to twenty-four years in prison.

There was no DNA to save him from his long incarceration. Yet, six years later, Long was freed after his Legal Aid attorneys spent two years convincing the Queens district attorney and Judge Joseph Golia that he'd been erroneously convicted.

The only thing that had changed was that a police officer later remembered being told something at the time that corroborated Long's alibi, adding that he hadn't thought it important enough to pass on to detectives. After Long and his alibi witness also passed polygraph tests, the judge ruled in his favor.

"It has become evident that Mr. Long was not the person who committed the crime at issue," the judge said in his opinion. "There are rare cases when strict adherence to the law fails to meet the needs that justice demands. Indeed, while fairness is always just, justice is not always fair. Such a matter is the case of Lee Long. . . . The confidence of the public in the criminal justice system will only be enhanced by setting an innocent man free."

As he walked out of supreme court, Long said he had never lost his faith in God. "I just prayed every day," he said. "I have no anger for anyone."

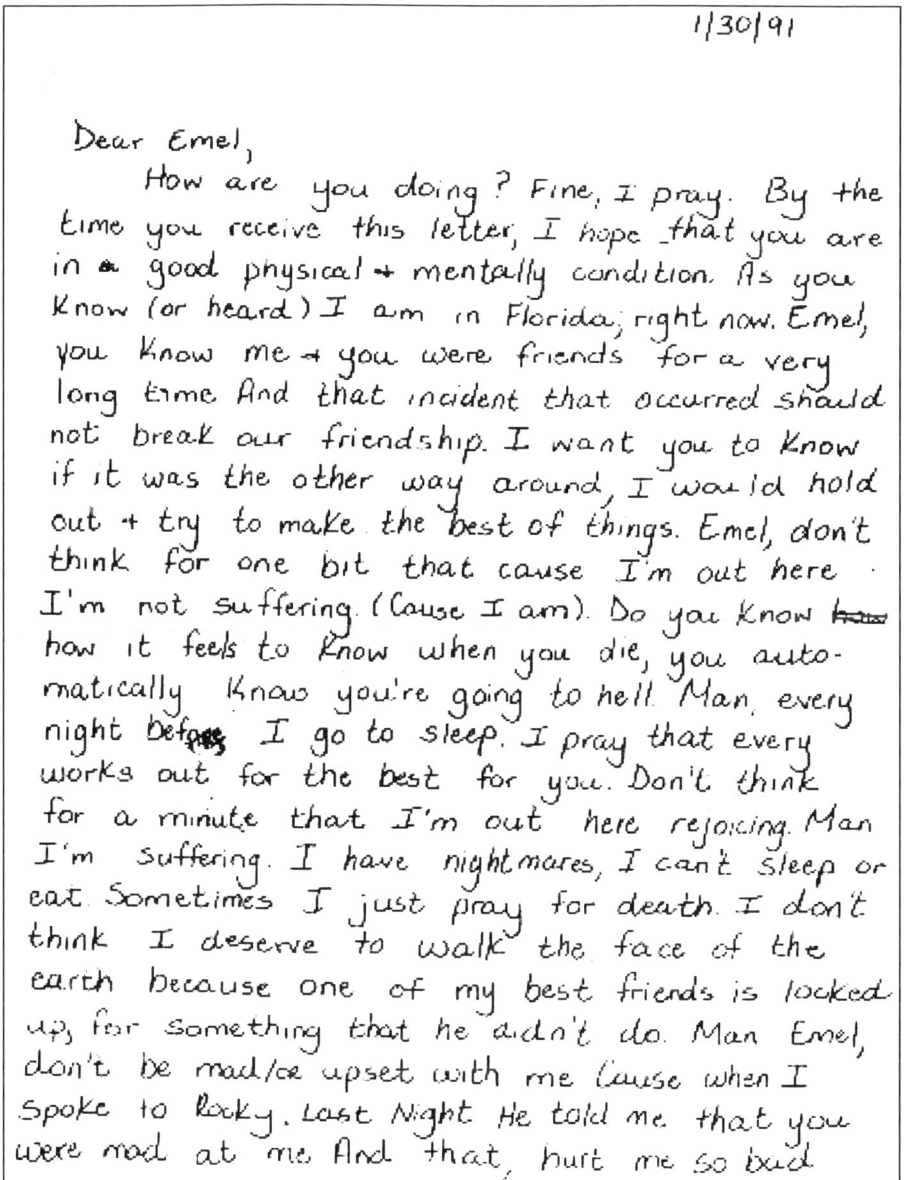

1/30/91

Dear Emel,

How are you doing? Fine, I pray. By the time you receive this letter, I hope that you are in a good physical + mentally condition. As you know (or heard) I am in Florida, right now. Emel, you know me + you were friends for a very long time. And that incident that occurred should not break our friendship. I want you to know if it was the other way around, I would hold out + try to make the best of things. Emel, don't think for one bit that cause I'm out here I'm not suffering. (Cause I am). Do you know how it feels to know when you die, you automatically know you're going to hell. Man, every night before I go to sleep. I pray that every works out for the best for you. Don't think for a minute that I'm out here rejoicing. Man I'm suffering. I have nightmares, I can't sleep or eat. Sometimes I just pray for death. I don't think I deserve to walk the face of the earth because one of my best friends is locked up, for something that he didn't do. Man Emel, don't be mad/or upset with me cause when I spoke to Rocky. Last Night He told me that you were mad at me. And that, hurt me so bad

Letter to McDowell. *Courtesy of Emel McDowell.*

that you feel this way towards me I feel like this if whoever didn't do what they had to do, all three of us (Me, you, Troy) probably would have been dead. And you know I'm not the type that will turn my back on a friend. So try to get all those negative thoughts out of your mind & remember I'm always here for you & my phone # on Greene is still the same ████████████ I'm not out here hiding. I'm in Florida, so I can try to get a peace in my mind & soul. Cause on the block certain people kept pressuring me to do things that would not help me or you. So now I'm out here In Florida striving to be the best person I know how to be, and I want you to remember you have a friend that's still concern about you & A friend that can not rest until you are set free.

Yours Truly,
BARON

P.S. Try & keep my letters confidental because I don't want for our business to gets in the street

    P.S If you need something write in & I'll try to send it to you.

Kings

"Don't Think I'm out Here Rejoicing"

On October 27, 1990, Emel McDowell, age seventeen, was attending a "wilding" party at a Bedford-Stuyvesant dancehall with his girlfriend and other friends. A fight broke out and a gang of twelve to fifteen youths started beating and stomping one of the guests. Jonathan Powell was shot and died en route to the hospital, and another youth was wounded.

McDowell was later stopped by the police, interviewed, and put through a lineup at the station house. Based on the eyewitness identification, he was arrested and charged with the killing. On February 18, 1992, he was convicted of second-degree murder and criminal possession of a weapon. Judge Thaddeus Owens sentenced him to twenty-two years to life.

Subsequent investigation by the defense suggested that somebody else committed the murder.

Emel McDowell.
Courtesy of Emel McDowell.

McDowell received a letter in jail from a former acquaintance, Baron, who wrote, "I want you to know that if it was the other way around, I would hold out and try to make the best of things. Emel, don't think for one bit that cause I'm out here I'm not suffering. (Cause I am.) . . . Don't think for a minute that I'm out here rejoicing. . . . I don't think I deserve to walk the face of the earth because one of my best friends is locked up, for something that he didn't do. Man Emel, don't be mad/or upset with me."

Another youth, Jadon, offered an affidavit on April 23, 1992, that Baron had run up to him after the incident and attempted to hand him a gun, saying, "I just hit this kid, take this around the corner."

Another participant at the party, Trevor, who had been only four-teen years old at the time of the incident, also gave a sworn statement that he had helped stand guard while he saw one of his friends, Baron, shoot Powell in the chest. Trevor swore in his affidavit that McDowell was not at the scene of the shooting. Trevor said he gave his eyewitness account about the shooting to the original attorney of record, but he

wasn't called as a witness at the trial because he had a pending criminal case.

With McDowell incarcerated since 1991 and not expected to get out until June of 2013, several advocates, including staff at Centurion Ministries and a private investigator, are still trying to help him gain a reversal of his wrongful conviction. But he lacks money to support his defense. He did not commit the murder.

Los Angeles

SNAFU

In October 1993, Los Angeles police arrested a mentally ill homeless man on a park bench, for failure to appear at a jaywalking hearing. Without bothering to check his fingerprints or mug shots against their criminal history database, they identified him as a fugitive, Robert Sanders, a convicted embezzler who had absconded from a New York prison work-release program. New York state investigators came and escorted the man from California to Greenhaven Correctional Facility in Dutchess County, a maximum-security prison housing murderers and other long-termers. They did not verify his identity.

The prisoner kept saying he was Kerry Sanders, not Robert Sanders, but corrections authorities refused to believe him. He told them he'd been raped by an inmate, but they ignored that too. Sanders was handled as just another crazy convict.

However, in October 1995, federal officials apprehended the real Robert Sanders on a drug charge in Cleveland, and further checking quickly showed that the man in Greenhaven prison actually was Kerry Sanders. Kerry's mother, Mary Lee, had been trying to find her son since his sudden disappearance two years earlier, but the Los Angeles Police Department (LAPD) had continually told her his whereabouts were unknown. When he finally turned up on his way out of a New York prison, she hired a civil rights lawyer in Los Angeles. The attorney filed a federal civil rights lawsuit against California and New York authorities.

Everybody denied liability, and a parade of criminal justice officials connected with the case refused to accept any responsibility for how they'd treated Kerry Saunders.

Sanders had told Dr. Edward Y. Chung, Greenhaven's staff psychiatrist, more than seventy-five times over a two-year period that he didn't know why he was in prison. But Chung said in his deposition, "He should say, 'Thank you, for two years you guys treated me very nicely.'"

But when Los Angeles authorities settled their civil suit for $290,000, New York State agreed to pay $3.25 million, and Corrections

Kerry Saunders. *New York State Department of Correctional Services.*

Commissioner Glenn Goord promised to issue written letters of apology to Kerry Sanders and his mother.

Nobody required the corrections department to discipline anyone or adopt new safegaurds.

Queens

Brother's Keeper

Gerald Harris had earned strong reviews as a Golden Gloves boxing finalist, but in January 1992 he was charged with robbery in Queens, based solely on an eyewitness identification.

Five days into his trial, the court received a letter from Gerald's brother, Harold, claiming that he and others, not including Gerald, had committed the robberies. But the court kept the jury from learning about this letter, and Harold was convicted of a narcotics offense and sentenced to twenty-five years to life in South Carolina. Brother Gerald, meanwhile, was found guilty and sentenced to nine to eighteen years in prison.

Gerald's former boxing trainer, Bob Jackson, and other supporters insisted he was innocent. Stories by columnist Denis Hamill of the New

(*Left to right*) Smallman, Harris, Hellerstein, and Jackson.
Courtesy of William Hellerstein.

York *Daily News* and basic case documentation helped convince Professor William Hellerstein of Brooklyn Law School that Gerald had been wrongly convicted of his brother's crime. To make sure, Hellerstein interrogated him and arranged for a polygraph examination. The results indicated that Harris was telling the truth. But then Hellerstein had to convince the court.

Working with Jackson and defense attorney Philip Smallman, Hellerstein took his evidence to the Queens County district attorney, who eventually decided to reinvestigate and petitioned the court to reopen the case. (The Queens DA is the most responsive in the state, dating back to the days of Frank O'Connor.)

In November 2000, Justice Randall Eng conducted hearings that included testimony by several key witnesses. Ultimately, the Queens DA consented to the motion to vacate Gerald Harris's conviction. On December 15, 2000, Harris was set free in time to spend Christmas with his family for the first time in eight years.

Denis Hamill, *Daily News* Columnist

Three times a week, reporter Denis Hamill writes his column for the *Daily News*, and occasionally the subject involves somebody he contends is wrongly imprisoned.

One story, about boxer Gerald Harris, helped get the Queens DA to reopen the case and ultimately contributed toward Harris's exoneration. "I can't stand the idea of somebody going to the can for something they didn't do," says Hamill. "I also know that as a writer, you can get burned, like Norman Mailer or William Buckley, when it turns out that you were wrong. You're a jury of one when you're a columnist."

Hamill says he stuck his neck out for Harris after the boxer's former trainer vouched for his innocence. "Bob Jackson is an honest, conservative guy, who happens to have worked as a hack in Sing Sing, so I took him seriously," says Hamill. "I also got the same reading from a guy I respect and grew up with—Gerald's lawyer, Phil Smallman, who is a former ADA. I like to think that I'm equipped with a sort of Brooklyn street polygraph, and after interviewing Harris and reading the trial record, I decided to go to bat for him."

When Harris was released from prison, Hamill rode home with him in the car. "It was a wonderful thing to watch, but it made me angry," the columnist says. "Poor guy just wanted to stand in his back yard—it was almost more than he could handle. It made me feel like this whole injustice never should have happened."

Kings

A Mother's Agony

In 1989, Lamont Branch was convicted of murdering a drug dealer in Kings County and sentenced to twenty-five years to life. The Appellate Division and the Court of Appeals upheld his conviction.

From the time of his arrest, however, Lamont's mother and sister told prosecutors they had the wrong person, and Lamont's look-alike brother, Lorenzo, even confessed to the crime on videotape, saying he had killed the man in self-defense. As in the Gerald Harris case noted earlier, Lamont's postconviction lawyer tried to get the DA to administer a polygraph test, but the prosecution refused. So the defense went ahead and commissioned its own lie detector exam. On May 22, 1997, polygraph expert Joseph Barry tested Lamont Branch in prison and concluded that he was telling the truth when he denied any involvement in the shooting.

Despite the presentation of compelling new evidence of his factual innocence, the trial judge rejected the defense motion for a new trial, citing Lorenzo Branch's manipulation of the legal system. Lorenzo didn't come forward until his brother's direct appeal was exhausted, and then he claimed self-defense and invoked his Fifth Amendment privilege on the witness stand when questioned about the homicide. The judge ruled that because the videotaped statement would not be admissible if a new trial were granted, it could not be used to vacate the conviction.

Thirteen years into his imprisonment, defense lawyers and the family continued to work to free Lamont Branch. Sara Bennett of the Legal Aid Society succeeded in getting the case back in court. In early 2002, both brothers appeared at a hearing in state supreme court. Lorenzo testified that he, not his brother, had accidentally done the killing, and a former prosecution witness testified that he had lied when he had identified Lamont as running away from the murder scene. After numerous hearings and extensive media coverage, his conviction was finally overturned and he was freed.

Prison Is a Place

From a letter to the author from Lamont Branch, 90-A-7206, Shawangunk Correctional Facility, dated 10/3/01:

Prison is a place where the first prisoner you see looks like an All-American College student and you are surprised. Later, you are disgusted because people on the outside still have the same prejudices about prisoners that you used to have.

Prison is a place where you write letters and cannot think of anything to say. Where you gradually write fewer and fewer letters, then stop writing altogether.

Prison is a place where you find gray hairs in your head, or where you find your hair starting to disappear. It is a place where you get false teeth, stronger glasses, aches and pains you never felt before. It is a place where you grow old and worry about it.

Prison is a place where you hate with clenched teeth, where you want to beat, hit, kick and scratch the person who put you in there. Then you wonder if the Psychologists know what they are talking about when they say you actually hate yourself.

Prison is a place where you learn that nobody needs you, that the outside world goes on without you being there.

Prison is a place where you can go for months without feeling the touch of a human hand, where you can go for months without hearing kind words such as I love you, I miss you, etc. It is a place where friendships are shallow and you know it.

Prison is a place where you hear about a friend's divorce, and you didn't know that he was married. It is a place where you hear about your neighbor's kids graduating from school and you didn't even know that they had kids who started school.

Prison is a place where you feel sorry for yourself. All of a sudden you're mad for feeling disgusted and then you try to mentally change the subject, but it sticks with you.

Prison is a place where you lose respect for the law. That is because you see it raw, naked, twisted, bent, ignored and blown out of proportion to suit the people who enforce it.

Prison is a place where you are smarter than the parole hearing board and staff. Because you know which guys will go straight and which ones will not. You are wrong just as often as the parole board members are, but you never admit it and neither do they.

Prison is a place where you wait for a promised visit. When it doesn't come, you worry about a car accident. When you find out the reason your visit didn't come, you are glad because it was not serious—and disappointed because such a little thing could keep them from coming to see you.

Prison is a place where you forget the sounds of a baby's cry. You forget the sounds of a dog's bark, or even the sounds of a dial tone from a telephone.

Prison is a place where a letter from home or a lawyer can be like a telegram from the war department. When you see it lying on your bed, you are afraid to open it. But you do anyway and usually you won't end up angry or disappointed.

Prison is a place where you see men you do not admire and wonder if you are like them. It is a place where you strive to remain civilized, but where you lose ground and know it.

Prison is a place where if you are married, you watch your marriage die. It is a place where you learn that absence does not make the heart grow fonder, and you start blaming your wife for wanting to live with a real man instead of a fading memory. But it is also a place where support can make things grow back once again.

Prison is a place where you go to bed before you are feeling tired. Where you pull the blankets over your head when you are not cold. It is a place where you escape by reading, playing cards, checkers, chess, or just going mad.

Prison is a place where you can really fool yourself. A place where you promise yourself you will live a better life when you leave. Sometimes you do, but more often you don't.

Prison is a place where you can go out someday, then you wonder how can everyone else be so calm when you are excited. Your bus driver does twenty-five miles an hour, and you want to tell him to slow down, but you don't, because you don't want to look foolish.

Prison is a place where prisoners are always wrong about matters, even though they are 100% correct. It is a place that would be foolish to listen to somebody who made one mistake in their life.

Prison is a place where the unknown gets the authority to do what they want, when they want, who they want, and where they want, even if it means costing the life of another.

Prison is a place where nothing comes fair. It is a place where you must do by all means necessary to survive and stand tall before someone pulls you back down.

Prison is a place where the least intelligence is used, whether it's by staff or Prisoner. It's a place where most of the Prisoners have low reading and math levels, and the Staff only needs a GED to work. It is best to go the wrong route than the right route to solve problems in prison.

Prison is a place where you could get delivered back to your family in a pine box, and all your medical records will have vanished or been altered. It is a place where Administration is responsible for your safety and well-being. So they will do whatever must be done to clear themselves from all legal matters.

Prison is a place where the Officers are supposedly known as the good guys, who are really the bad guys, they just haven't got caught for wrong-doings. And if they were, they have a Union and fellow bad Officers to assist them. It's a place where the Officers are really the gang-bangers because they move within groups to assault Prisoners for no reason needed.

Prison is a place where you can't find a thing called "UNITY." Because Prisoners are divided up into groups by the Administration, and this is planting "negative" into the minds of the Prisoners where they feel the group they belong to is superior to the next group. They also have "Prisoners" and "inmates" trying to strive for a different cause. They make us all into a different kind of "Nation of People." This is their terminology of "Divide and Conquer."

Prison is a place where it is easy to get into, but hard to get out of. A place where a little mistake in a person's life can mean "Eternal Pain."

Prison is a place where racism is a big part of everyday life and it is upheld by the racism capital, "THE ADMINISTRATION." Officers against Prisoners, White against Black, Blacks against Latinos, Latinos against West Indians, and the list goes on. Very few mix with others than their own.

Prison is a place where *you* are not known by your name, you are just a number. It is a place where you get nothing without that number, such as mail, packages, phone calls, commissary, etc., and the list goes on.

Prison is a place where you are told when to eat, sleep, wake up, shower, and use the bathroom. Meanwhile, they want you to be more responsible for your life, but they don't let you have the liberty to do so.

Prison is a place where they take your personal money and call it a surcharge, restitution, encumbrance, or lagged payroll, but if you take money, it's called "robbery." They will even take your money and call it a "HARMLESS ERROR."

Prison is a place where people idolize their job making 17 cents per hour, and while they were on the streets, they would take a job making minimum wage and work less hard.

Prison is a place where people get sliced up daily by a razor, which is considered contraband. It is a place where each Prisoner is given two razors upon their entering the prison. Then they wonder why there are so many slicings.

Prison is a place where they (staff) can take anything from you, and it's legal, and the only thing you can do is write and hope for an answer. It is a place where the power is abused and you try to make a change but can't.

Prison is a place where they use experimental drugs on you and it's OK. But when you want to experiment with drugs, they lock you up and give you more time.

Prison is a place where you hear some of the most unbelievable stories. It is a place where everybody was a big-time drug dealer, killer, robber, etc., but nobody was the victim or user.

Prison is a place where there is only one person known by every Black family member, whether it's a member or friend. Every Black family has a member of their family or a friend in prison. It is a place where 1 of every

4 Black males resides at. And 1 of every 3 is paroled, on probation or locked up.

Prison is a place where 8 different Federal Court Judges found 28 Correctional Officers (Clinton C.F.) guilty of assaulting Prisoners in such a severe manner that damages ranged from $18,000 to $40,000 per beaten Prisoner were awarded. Although the Judges called the beatings unnecessary and "savage," all the sued officers remained employed in different Prisons. Some of them were even awarded for a good job.

Prison is a place where Prisoners who allege abuse are harshly punished for lying when telling the truth, while the abusive Officer can quite literally "get away with murder." It is a place where if an Officer is convicted of murdering a Prisoner, he will be granted parole after serving 3 years, or will never see a day of incarceration.

Prison is a place where the State made it increasingly difficult for a Prisoner to bring their complaints to court. New York's Governor G. Pataki has vetoed the entire budget (1998) approved for Prisoners Legal Services of New York.

Prison is a place where laboratory reports showed a "high level of human fecal matter, nitrogen, and pesticides were found in the drinking water." It is a place where things like this go unnoticed. That is why all Officers have their own water.

Prison is a place where they will issue an Executive Order banning face-to-face media interviews with Prisoners and prohibiting Prisoners from sending confidential mail to representatives of the media.

Prison is a place where they have sharp cutbacks in Prisoners' health care, counseling, vocational, and educational programs. It is a place that does this to take away what modest privileges Prisoners have and replace them with idleness. Yet, they want to still call Prison a place for rehabilitation. It is a place where this has historically led to violence and the level of overcrowding in prison today will only exacerbate the level of conflict.

Prison is a place that has witnessed the dismissal of 130 drug treatment counselors, 93 vocational instructors, 35 academic teachers, 50 recreational staff, 45 library clerks, and 45 work release counselors in the year 1996-1997. Several prisons have eliminated rehabilitation program classes on repairs of air conditioners, refrigerators, automobiles, radio and television repairs, auto mechanics, tailoring, masonry, carpentry, painting, sheet metal, business education, and all college programs.

Prison is a place that is storing Prisoners as if they were in the slave ships, in double bunked cells, whereas each cell is the size of a standard bathroom in a family's apartment (6' x 8'). This is opposed by Prisoners and Officers, but the State of New York still allows it.

Prison is a place where they don't care about your well-being. It is a place where there is often little regard for a person's safety. In one situation, Prisoners spent 45 hours removing asbestos which was hanging from the pipes, and bagged it for disposal, without any type of protective clothing provided for the Prisoners or for the Officers who supervised them.

Prison is a place where the phone company has extorted high rates from Prisoners' families and friends. It is a place where if you live 1 mile away, a call can cost you about $1.00 per minute.

Prison is a place where Politicians often reinforce such hysteria and pressure prison officials to eliminate "perks" such as weight lifting. The rationale espoused is that criminals bulking up will make them more dangerous. Yet, these same legislators also support them "boot camp prisons" which increase Prisoners' physical stamina.

Prison is a place where Officers, in private conversations, acknowledge that they have witnessed brutal, corrupt, or racist behavior by some of their fellow Officers. Yet they remain silent, they explain, because they would otherwise be subjected to the same kind of retaliation and ostracism that Prisoners who report wrongdoing of other prisoners have received.

Prison is a place that has taken jobs out of your community and placed them into these trailer park communities. It is a place that has taken away the number of people in your Census and added them to other communities making them stronger.

Prison is a place that is designed to destroy all family values. It is a place that discourages you from seeing your loved one. So it is up to you to fight back and say, "You're not destroying my family."

Prison is a place that kidnaps and houses over 2 million Black men here in America. It is a place that is also starting to kidnap and house our Black sisters too. Since 1992 women in prison has risen 275%.

Prison is a place that is big business for the State's economy. The Federal government pays about $30,000 to house each prisoner. If they was really interested in people not coming to jail, they could give a person in need $18,000 to get on his feet, then invest the rest into education. So this shows that they are not interested in the future of our youth's education, just lock them up and collect the money.

Oneida

The Price of Refusing to Plead Guilty

Two years after the 1973 brutal killing of a seventeen-year-old gas station attendant in Sherrill, New York, police in North Carolina questioned a young lesbian about the crime and her association with a gay man who was considered the chief suspect. Patsy Kelly Jarrett, age twenty-one, readily cooperated and told them what she knew without bothering to contact a lawyer. Although she hadn't admitted participating in the crime, four months later she and her former acquaintance were charged with robbery and murder.

Patsy Kelly Jarrett. *Courtesy of Abbe Smith.*

Police had extensive evidence against the former male companion. But the main evidence against Jarrett was that, two years after the crime, a witness had picked her picture from a police photo array as "possibly the accomplice" he had seen at the gas station with the male killer shortly after the murder. Jarrett's photo was the only one of the twelve displayed that carried a "Sheriff's Department" label.

Represented by an inexperienced court-appointed attorney who had never handled a murder case, Jarrett refused to plead guilty to felony murder in exchange for a reduced sentence, and the pair went on trial in 1977. Both defendants were convicted of robbery and murder and sentenced to twenty-five years to life in prison.

In 1982 her codefendant submitted an affidavit saying that he had committed the murder with someone other than Jarrett, but he refused to say who it was. Jarrett continued to insist she was innocent. A prison escape added even more time to her sentence.

In 1986, after nearly ten years in custody, her petition for a writ of habeas corpus was granted by U.S. District Judge David Edelstein, on the grounds that the identification at trial was the product of an unduly suggestive procedure and had no independent basis. Shortly after the writ was granted, Jarrett was offered what was essentially a time-served sentence in exchange for a guilty plea. However, she refused to plead, saying she was innocent. When the U.S. Court of Appeals for the Second Circuit reversed the district court's decision, she remained in prison on the original sentence.

Her current lawyer and friend for several years, Professor Abbe Smith of Georgetown Law Center, who worked on Jarrett's case as a law student, says Jarrett has exhausted all her legal remedies except executive clemency, but she is still trying to prove her innocence. They contend that the killer's likely accomplice was a male acquaintance who later died of AIDS. Despite the lack of corroborating evidence against Jarrett, and although she has passed a polygraph test confirming her account, she remains in prison and is now one of the longest-serving female inmates in New York State. She is also innocent and devoutly religious.

The Woodbourne Word (Prison Newspaper), November/December 2000: "A Father's Hope, a Daughter's Dream"

By Ruben Montalvo

I am pretty sure that you may have heard this story. Some may believe it, others may not. However, it is a fact. I am in prison for a crime I did not commit. The effort to prove my innocence fell short of the challenge, so here I am. After a trial by jury, I was convicted of murder in the second degree and ultimately sentenced to 15 years to life.

At the time of my arrest, I was sixteen years of age. Still in high school, my girlfriend and I were expecting our first child. It was an important stage in my life. Although young, I was looking forward to taking on the responsibilities of fatherhood. I wasn't alone in my position. Several of my friends and classmates were already dads. Babies having babies was a common practice in the hood.

Then, suddenly, my life took a turn for the worst.

On a fairly warm October morning in 1987, my friend J.R. and I were chilling in my bedroom when my mother came knocking on my door. She told me to check out the commotion in front of the building. I went to the window and saw dozens of police cars out front. The whole precinct must've been there, detectives, uniformed officers, and I think even a SWAT team had been dispatched. I had no idea what was going on. But I knew somebody was in serious trouble. Moments later, someone was banging on our apartment door.

"Open the door, it's the police!" shouted somebody from the other side.

My mother and I looked at one another. JR's bottom jaw fell to his chest. Not knowing what was going on, my mother refused to open the door. She was afraid and began to cry. I insisted that she open the door. Maybe we were being evacuated for some reason. As the door squeaked open, a flood of cops rushed in and tackled me to the floor. A boot pressed my face to the carpet as Dan-O read the Miranda rights before booking me for murder.

My life made a drastic change.

Suddenly, I was a murderer. In that instant and the time that followed, I was deprived of my childhood, adolescence, and the right to pursue my dreams when I was falsely accused and convicted of homicide. The judge knew, but his hands were tied. The jury had spoken. The best that he could do was sentence me to the minimum of fifteen years to life. My loved ones suffered. My daughter is growing up wondering who I am and when I will be home. My wife has replaced me and my friends are no longer my friends. Still, I could not fold under the pressure. I had to make do with what was done.

Coming to prison was a new experience for me. I was bitter. I had no guidance. I was lost and now was living in the belly of the beast. The reality: I was *here* and *there was nothing I could do about it*. All appeals were eventually denied and the little faith that I may have had in the courts was gone. Fifteen years. Fifteen long years before parole consideration. What was I going to do with the time?

In the process of maturing in prison, I had to apply myself. Somehow I needed to make the best of this and get my life back on track. I fell back from a lot of the abnormal nonsense that's normal prison issues. They served no purpose toward the goals I set and was looking to achieve. I intended to take full advantage of my time and rehabilitate myself. Even though I was innocent of this crime, there was a degree of criminal mentality I still had to deal with. I was angry to the point of becoming violent, and I had to deal with that anger. My destiny was to become a better man than I was in the past.

I believe that I have learned to deal with the anger that was bubbling up inside of me. If I was to find myself in a situation that most would normally answer with violence, I needed to know if and how I could handle the scenario. I didn't want to begin taking matters into my own hands. The pain of this experience gave me all the incentive in the world to do things the right way. Getting an education, maintaining a job, and living a normal productive life in society is what's become important to me.

In this development, fatherhood grew exceptionally important to me. Half my life I've spent isolated. From a teenage boy, I grew up to become a man on my own in prison. Without having any role models, I had to learn the responsibilities of fatherhood on my own. I asked questions. I crawled through programs and spoke with female employees and volunteers who were mothers. I spoke with prisoners, staff, and male volunteers who were fathers. I learned the dos and don'ts, right and wrongs. I learned to be fair, but firm. I came to understand that I am a living example of what becomes important to my child.

I also know what it's like to feel hopelessness, condemnation, and now, rehabilitation. But I need social awareness. I need to know what it's like to have a job, become head of my household, support my family. I've never had to pay bills, rent, and shop for food, clothing, nor budget for the phone bill. My mother took care of all that. I was a high school student.

But now I am a proud father of a twelve-year-old girl, a daughter who's counted days, weeks, months and years in wait for her father. She always tells me she needs me. I need her too. Our relationship has been established through visits, phone calls, letters and pictures. Those are the things that weather the storms, help us through bad times. By the grace of God, we hold a bond strong enough to hold us down. Fifteen irreplaceable years will have gone by.

Then I'll see the parole board.

It's been my observation from what I've seen and read in the newspapers that parole denial is almost assured. Regardless of my innocence, the fact remains that I am convicted of a violent offense. And violent offenders are not being paroled, especially at the first parole board appearance. Individual circumstances don't seem to matter. So what do I have to look forward to? What do I tell my daughter after she's waited this long, remained so hopeful, took pride in every certificate and award I've sent home? No matter how qualified or fit I may be with regard to the criteria for parole release, it appears parole denial is preordained.

The majority of violent offenders are being held until expiration of their conditional release dates. A conditional release date, commonly referred to as a CR date, is a legal provision requiring an inmate's release after serving two-thirds of his maximum sentence. At this time, the parole board no longer has discretion in releasing the inmate and unless there is a loss of good time credits, then the inmate must be released.

Unfortunately, I do not have a conditional release date. I am a lifer. After having to serve fifteen years, my fate remains in the hands of the parole board indefinitely.

So is it with my daughter's hopes to see her father come home.

Bronx

Rearranging the Evidence to Fit

In 1987 three men, including Jose Rivera, were drinking in a New York City park when one of them made vulgar remarks to some passing girls. After friends of the girls returned to the scene, Rivera stabbed one of the strangers (Peter Ramirez) and three others.

Months later, accompanied by some other youths, Ramirez retaliated and attacked and killed Rivera on a Bronx street in front of the victim's wife and son. Ramirez told police he had killed Rivera but refused to identify his accomplices. The victim's grieving wife identified the attackers as Ramirez and two others—Ruben Montalvo and Jose Morales. All three were charged with murder.

Ramirez told his attorney that Montalvo and Morales were innocent of the crime. Then he committed suicide. But the trial judge later refused to allow his purported suicide note or any testimony by Ramirez's mother to be admitted as evidence in the case against Montalvo and Morales.

Both men refused an offer by the Bronx DA that would have allowed them to spend two years in prison in exchange for a guilty plea on reduced charges.

At trial, the DA shocked the defense by alleging that Montalvo and Morales, not Ramirez, had been the main attackers. The victim's wife also changed her testimony to implicate Morales as having accompanied Ramirez at an earlier confrontation a few days before the killing. When all was said and done, Morales and Montalvo were convicted of second-degree murder.

Just before the sentencing, a youth named Jesus Fornes went to the families of the convicted men and said that he and his uncle—not Morales and Montalvo—had served as Ramirez's accomplices. Fornes also told this to his appeals lawyer, Anthony Servino, and spoke privately about it with his parish priest, Father Joseph Towle. In court, however, Fornes invoked the Fifth Amendment, and the judge ruled that Morales and Montalvo were not entitled to a new trial. He sentenced them both to fifteen years to life.

Morales and Montalvo languished in prison. In 1997 their situation worsened when Fornes died. But they received help from researchers at Centurion Ministries, the not-for-profit organization in Princeton, New Jersey, that investigates wrongful conviction cases. Centurion staffers prepared extensive write-ups on the case and aided other investigators. Prison reformer Joel Freedman of Canandaigua also took up the matter and got some big-time journalists to look into the case. The newspaper stories in Morales and Montalvo's favor began to pile up.

In July 2001, a horde of New York City news reporters, photographers, and television crews descended as Father Towle submitted an affidavit to District Judge Denny Chin as part of the federal habeas corpus petition. In it he said Fornes had admitted his role in the killing but insisted that Morales and Montalvo were innocent. The priest said he had urged Fornes to tell the authorities, but Fornes had later decided not to testify.

Bronx assistant district attorney Allen P. W. Karen tried to prevent Towle from testifying, claiming that any such admission by Fornes had occurred during a confidential "confession," and hence it was privileged and could not be allowed as evidence. However, the Archdiocese of New York contended the discussion had not been a formal church confession, and thus it was not privileged. As a result, the judge refused to exclude the priest's account of Fornes's statements.

Judge Chin also received testimony from a Legal Aid lawyer who said he had advised Fornes not to incriminate himself at the time because he didn't expect Morales and Montalvo to be convicted.

Judge Chin characterized the evidence against the two men as "incredibly thin." Then he said, "I don't know what the jury was thinking. When you look at all the evidence, I cannot imagine why the jury would convict." Chin reversed Morales's conviction and ordered him released.

A few days later he did the same for Montalvo. Chin rebuked the prosecutors for trying to keep Montalvo in prison. "I can't understand why the district attorney's office is fighting this," he said. "I would urge the [Bronx DA's] office to give this a good hard look instead of worrying about protecting a conviction."

Advocate Joel Freedman

Longtime activist and prisoners' rights advocate Joel Freedman retired from his job as a social worker with the Veterans Administration in 1994, after a judge ordered him reinstated following his firing for being a whistle-blower.

"The experience of being falsely accused and facing dismissal on trumped-up charges made me appreciate more fully what it must be like to suffer imprisonment and everything else that goes with it," he says, "and from that point I vowed that when I was cleared I would go to bat for people wrongfully accused." Since then, Freedman has researched and helped publicize numerous cases involving prisoners who claim to be wrongly incarcerated.

Freedman, who lives in upstate Ontario County, spends much of his time attending trials, conducting interviews, chatting with law

Joel Freedman and friend. *Courtesy of Joel Freedman.*

enforcement personnel, and writing columns and letters for various local newspapers and *Justicia*, the Rochester-based newsletter of the Judicial Process Commission. He also supplies information to lawyers and investigative reporters who work with him on cases. Some of his efforts have contributed to reversals of inmates' convictions.

"I have no ax to grind and no desire to see guilty people get off," he says. "But I do want to see justice. And when I see somebody being treated unfairly, I try to get involved."

Complainant's Name - Last, First, M.I.
P/S/N/Y/

Victim's Name - If Different

Witness No. 1	Last Name, First, M.I.		Address, Include City, State, Zip		Apt. No.
	Home Telephone	Business Telephone	Position/Relationship to Victim	Date of Birth	

Witness No. 2	Last Name, First, M.I.		Address, Include City, State, Zip		Apt. No.
	Home Telephone	Business Telephone	Position/Relationship to Victim	Date of Birth	

AREA WITHIN BOX FOR DETECTIVE/LATENT FINGERPRINT OFFICER ONLY

| Comp. Interviewed ☐ Yes ☐ No | In Person ☐ | By Phone ☐ | Date | Time | Results: Same As Comp. Report - Different (Explain in Details) ☐ ☐ |
| Witness Interviewed ☐ Yes ☐ No | In Person ☐ | By Phone ☐ | Date | Time | Results: Same as Comp. Report - Different (Explain in Details) ☐ ☐ |

Canvass Conducted ☐ Yes ☐ No   If Yes - Make Entry in Body Re: Time, Date Names, Addresses, Results
Crime Scene Visited ☐ Yes ☐ No   If Yes - Make Entry in Details Re: Time, Date, Evidence Obtained

Complainant Viewed Photos ☐ Yes ☐ Refused ☐ Future   Results:

Witness Viewed Photos ☐ Yes ☐ Refused ☐ Future   Results:

Crime Scene Dusted ☐ Yes ☐ No   By (Enter Results in Details)
Crime Scene Photos ☐ Yes ☐ No   By (Enter Results in Details)

If Closing Case "No Results," Check Appropriate Box and State Justification in Details:
☐ C-1 Improper Referral   ☐ C-2 Inaccurate Facts   ☐ C-3 No Evidence/Can't ID   ☐ C-4 Uncooperative Complainant

DETAILS:

SUBJECT: RETURN OF DELISA CARTER DURHAM FROM CONNECTICT, AND VIDIO TAPED STATEMENTS.

1.   On 01/18/84 the undersigned and detective Alicia Parker # 22 drove Delisa Carter Durham from the Bristol Police Department to the office of the Connecticut State's Attorney's, at 95 Washington Street, Hartford Connecticut. There we were assisted by inspector Edmund A. Kozlowski.

2.   At approximately 10:45 A/M (01/18/84) Delisa Carter Durham appeared before Judge Quinn, and was turned over to the undersigned for transportation back to New York as per the material witness order.

3.   At approximately 15:45 hours (01/18/84) while at the office of the Queens District Attorney Delisa Carter Durham voluntarily submitted to an interview that was video taped. Present at that interview were A/D/A Thomas Russo, A/D/A Mark Furman, Detective John Boccone, D/I Joseph Salvo (the video operator), and the undersigned. During the course of the interview Delisa Carter Durham made statements implicating herself as the murderer, and additional statements were made exonerating Nathanial Carter of responsiblity for the murder.

4.   After having spoken with Judge Leahy, and due to the weather conditions (it was snowing) a decision was reached and the undersigned was directed to place Delisa Carter Durham in a hotel for the night.

5. RECOMMEND CASE REMAIN OPEN AND ACTIVE AT THIS TIME.

Reporting Officer's Rank - Signature - Command	Name Printed R. CULLEN	Tax Registry No. 852365	Supervisor's Signature	C.O.'s Initials

Police report admitting eyewitness perjury. *Courtesy of Lawrence Halford.*

3

Eyewitness Perjury

Things are often not as they seem. Sometimes the key eyewitness is intentionally lying—to protect himself/herself or someone else, or for some other purpose. This is another reason that eyewitness testimony must be carefully scrutinized before it is used as criminal evidence.

Queens

People v. Nathaniel Carter

In 1981, Nathaniel (Nate) Carter was arrested for the fatal stabbing of his former mother-in-law in Queens County, based exclusively on the testimony of his ex-wife, Delissa. Represented by a series of court-appointed counsel, Carter was convicted of murder and sentenced to twenty-five years to life. He was thirty-one years old.

There it might have remained, except that Lieutenant James Nelson of the Peekskill Police Department took an interest in the case against his childhood friend. Nelson brought his findings to Peekskill police commissioner Walter Kirkland, a law enforcement official known for his willingness to take an independent stand. After concluding that Carter hadn't committed the crime, Kirkland took the unusual step of going to

Crime scene. *Courtesy of Lawrence Halford.*

the Legal Aid Society of New York City on Carter's behalf. He convinced William E. Hellerstein of the Appeals Bureau to take up the case.

Working with investigator Ettore Perrazzo, Hellerstein and attorney Lawrence Halfond found ten witnesses to confirm Carter's alibi, which the police had never checked. They also arranged for Carter to take a lie detector test at Great Meadow Correctional Facility, and he passed it. All evidence pointed instead to his ex-wife. On June 28, 1983, the lawyers submit-

William E. Hellerstein. *Author's photo.*

ted an extensive memorandum to Queens district attorney John J. Santucci, laying out their case. It convinced the DA to order a reinvestigation.

Six months later, the parties appeared at a hearing held before Supreme Court Justice John J. Leahy—the judge who had sentenced

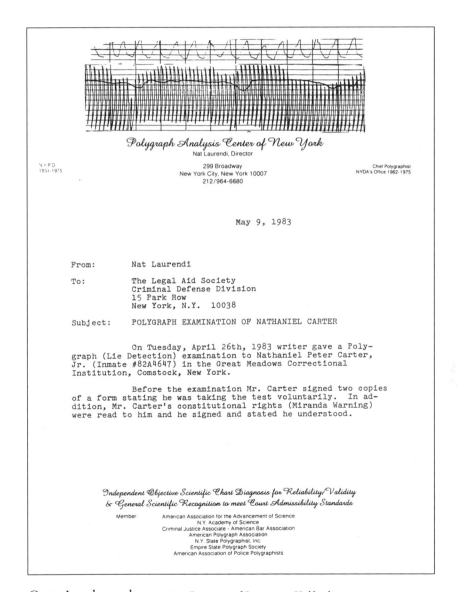

Polygraph Analysis Center of New York

Nat Laurendi, Director

N Y P D
1951-1975

299 Broadway
New York City, New York 10007
212/964-6680

Chief Polygraphist
NYDA's Office 1962-1975

May 9, 1983

From: Nat Laurendi

To: The Legal Aid Society
           Criminal Defense Division
           15 Park Row
           New York, N.Y. 10038

Subject: POLYGRAPH EXAMINATION OF NATHANIEL CARTER

          On Tuesday, April 26th, 1983 writer gave a Polygraph (Lie Detection) examination to Nathaniel Peter Carter, Jr. (Inmate #82A4647) in the Great Meadows Correctional Institution, Comstock, New York.

          Before the examination Mr. Carter signed two copies of a form stating he was taking the test voluntarily. In addition, Mr. Carter's constitutional rights (Miranda Warning) were read to him and he signed and stated he understood.

Independent Objective Scientific Chart Diagnosis for Reliability/Validity & General Scientific Recognition to meet Court Admissibility Standards

Member: American Association for the Advancement of Science
           N.Y. Academy of Science
           Criminal Justice Associate - American Bar Association
           American Polygraph Association
           N.Y. State Polygraphist, Inc.
           Empire State Polygraph Society
           American Association of Police Polygraphists

Carter's polygraph report. *Courtesy of Lawrence Halford.*

Carter. At the session, the prosecution announced that during their recent follow-up investigation, Carter's ex-wife, Delissa, had confessed to police that she, not Nate, had murdered her foster mother and then concocted the story. After hearing the testimony and apologizing to Carter for his wrongful conviction, Justice Leahy vacated the sentence and threw out the indictment against him.

Nate Carter was released after serving two and a half years in prison. In 1986 he received an out-of-court settlement of $450,000 for his wrongful conviction and imprisonment. He later moved to South Carolina.

An investigation by Philip Shenon of *The New York Times* found that police, prosecutors, and the court-appointed defense attorney had made many serious errors.

Delissa Carter was never prosecuted for the murder because the DA had granted her immunity for her earlier testimony.

GOVERNOR PATAKI, DO YOU REMEMBER NATHANIEL CARTER?

George Pataki with Nathaniel Carter, 1984.
Courtesy of New Yorkers against the Death Penalty.

Living Proof

Nate Carter had grown up playing basketball in Peekskill with George
Pataki in the 1960s, and Carter's chief appeals attorney, Will Hellerstein,
lived across the road from Pataki in Garrison. After Hellerstein proved
Carter had been wrongfully convicted of murder, then-mayor Pataki
showed up in Hellerstein's driveway one day. Hellerstein recalls saying,
"It's a good thing that New York doesn't have a death penalty, George,
because Nate might have been wrongfully sent to his death."

A few years later, Pataki's call for the reinstatement of capital punishment helped him unseat Mario Cuomo as governor. Carter urged his
old pal, George, to drop the death penalty idea in view of the dangers
revealed by his own case. But Governor Pataki went ahead and signed
the death penalty back into law.

Kings

Serial Liar

In 1988, Dana Garner went to the local police station in Brooklyn and
said he'd been kidnapped by four men, one of them Tim Crosby. Two
years later, Garner reported to police that he'd seen Jeffrey Blake murder
two men in a car in East New York. A week after that, Garner told the
same cops he'd witnessed Rubin Ortega murder a man and wound two
others. Based on Garner's testimony, Crosby, Blake, and Ortega were all
convicted and sentenced to long prison terms. None of them ever knew
that Garner had served as the star eyewitness in three unrelated serious
felony cases.

Jeffrey Blake

Garner told police that his girlfriend, Margaret Allen, had also witnessed
Blake kill the two men with an Uzi. But neither the prosecution nor the
defense ever called her to testify. There was there no corroborating evidence of Garner's account against Blake. Some of Garner's relatives even
swore that he was in North Carolina at the time of the crime, but the

Dana Garner. *Courtesy of the Legal Aid Society of New York.*

prosecutor did not believe them. During Blake's trial, Garner himself tried to recant his story, forcing an adjournment of the proceedings. But ADA Anthony Catalano privately threatened to make Garner submit to a polygraph exam or face criminal charges if he changed his account, until, ultimately, Garner was allowed to retake the stand to testify against Blake.

As a result, on March 26, 1991, Blake was convicted of the two murders. The judge sentenced him to thirty-six years to life.

Two years later, when Blake was appealing his conviction, Garner signed an affidavit for the defense and admitted on a defense videotape that he had never witnessed the slayings. But when it came time to say so in court, he pleaded the Fifth Amendment to avoid being prosecuted for perjury, and Blake's conviction was left undisturbed. Officials failed to conduct any further investigation.

When the Appellate Division, Second Department, and the Court of Appeals denied his appeals, Blake's appeals lawyer, Michelle Fox of the Legal Aid Society, recalls, "It was the most frustrating experience of my life." But Fox persisted. "I took up a slogan from the suffragettes to guide me—'Failure is impossible.'"

Fox tracked down Garner's former girlfriend in North Carolina and got her to sign an affidavit. The woman denied ever seeing any killings and said Garner had never mentioned them to her—poking a major hole in his story.

Michelle Fox. *Author's photo.*

"I kept calling the DA to tell him what I was finding," says Fox. "But he wouldn't return my calls or messages, so I put it in writing. Then I saw DA Charles Hynes publicly say, 'The last thing I want is an innocent person in jail.' So I used that remark to help get Bob Herbert of *The New York Times* interested."

Herbert is New York's most vigorous and influential journalist on behalf of the wrongly convicted. In 1998, he began writing columns about Blake's case. Suddenly, the DA's office agreed to meet with Fox.

After conducting an investigation, the executive ADA handling the case agreed to the granting of Blake's 440.10 motion and the vacating of his convictions, saying, "Mr. Garner's testimony is not something to be relied upon."

In October 1998, Justice Robert S. Kreindler vacated the conviction and dismissed the indictment. Garner, meanwhile, could not be prosecuted because the statute of limitations for perjury had expired.

Jeffrey Blake goes free. *Courtesy of the Legal Aid Society of New York.*

Tim Crosby (second from right) and family with lawyer Sara Bennet.
Courtesy of the Legal Aid Society of New York.

Tim Crosby

Tim Crosby had also been convicted based on Garner's word. As the Blake case unfolded, he was serving ten years to life for Garner's alleged kidnapping in April 1988.

Working next door to Michelle Fox at the Legal Aid Society, attorney Sara Bennett found out about Garner's lying in the Blake case. Bennett got Garner to sign an affidavit recanting his testimony against her client, Crosby.

Two of Crosby's codefendants had also signed affidavits, saying they had been pressured to implicate Crosby in their plea colloquy and that they had done so only as part of the bargain—not because he was guilty. Then Crosby passed a polygraph examination in which he denied any knowledge of the crime.

But the DA's office still dragged its feet. In December 1999, Justice Lewis L. Douglass ruled, "Dana Garner is a completely unreliable witness and where, as here, there is no other evidence connecting the defendant to the crime, I too grant the motion to vacate the judgment."

As soon as the judge ordered him released, Crosby bolted down the courthouse stairs and out of the building. It appeared that he had a good chance to win some money damages for wrongful conviction.

A few months later, Crosby was arrested, convicted, and sentenced to eighteen years for rape. His lawyer, Sara Bennett, felt devastated, wondering if she had made a mistake in championing him.

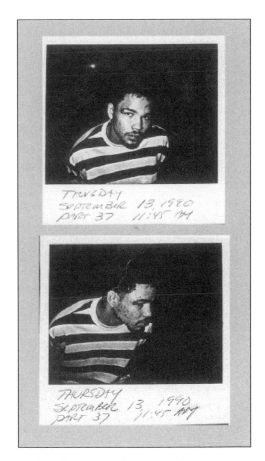

Rubin Ortega at the time of his arrest.
Courtesy of the Legal Aid Society of New York.

OFFICE OF THE DISTRICT ATTORNEY, KINGS COUNTY
RENAISSANCE PLAZA *at* 350 JAY STREET
BROOKLYN, N.Y. 11201–2908
(718) 250–2000

CHARLES J. HYNES
District Attorney

December 7, 1998
Andrew Hirschhorn, Esq.
1 Cross Island Plaza
Jamaica, New York 11422

Dear Mr. Hirschhorn:

The following is being provided to you, as the last counsel of record for Rubin Ortega.

On February 14, 1991, Rubin Ortega was convicted by jury verdict, of the crimes of Murder in the Second Degree and Criminal Possession of a Weapon in the Second Degree. On March 6, 1991, Rubin Ortega was sentenced to a term of 25 years to life on the Murder in the Second Degree conviction, and to a consecutive sentence of 5 to 15 years on the Criminal Possession of a Weapon conviction. This case involved the fatal shooting of Lionel Diaz and the wounding of Ricardo Betances and Angel Navaez on June 25, 1990.

On March 26, 1991, Jeffrey Blake was convicted by jury verdict, of the crime of Murder in the Second Degree (two counts) and Criminal Possession of a Weapon in the Second Degree. On May 23, 1991, Jeffrey Blake was sentenced to consecutive 18 years to life terms on the Murder in the Second Degree convictions, and to a concurrent sentence of 5 to 15 years on the Criminal Possession of a Weapon conviction. This case involved the fatal shooting of Everton Denny and Kenneth Felix on June 18, 1990.

An individual named Dana Garner was a witness called by the prosecution in each of the above cases. In each case Dana Garner testified to his observations of the criminal transactions, and in each case he identified the defendant as a principal in the respective crimes. In the case against Jeffrey

Blake, Dana Garner was the only witness who identified and inculpated Blake in the crime. In the case against Rubin Ortega, Dana Garner was one of two witnesses who identified and inculpated Ortega in the crime.

In October 28, 1998, the Office of the Kings County District Attorney made an application to the Justice of the Kings County Supreme Court who presided at the trial of Jeffrey Blake both to vacate the judgment of conviction, and to dismiss the indictment against Jeffrey Blake.

The application was made following an extensive investigation by this Office prompted by the presentation of information to this Office from the appellate attorney for Jeffrey Blake. The information, in substance, alleged that Dana Garner was not in New York City on June 18, 1990, the date of the crime, and, therefore, his testimony at the trial was false. Further, Dana Garner allegedly recanted his trial testimony in that matter in a videotaped statement made to colleagues of the appellate attorney.

This Office's investigation into the trial testimony of Dana Garner in the case of Jeffrey Blake has led to the conclusion that Dana Garner was not present in New York City on June 18, 1990, and, therefore, that he did not see the events about which he testified.

Among the people who were interviewed about that matter were Dana Garner's family members who provided information about his whereabouts on and before June 18, 1990. During the course of these interviews, information was received from Dana Garner's mother, which contradicted portions of his testimony at the trial of Rubin Ortega concerning the events of June 25, 1990. At that trial, Dana Garner testified, in substance, that his presence at the crime scene was the result of waiting for, and then meeting his mother, in the vicinity of the shooting, and also to certain events and activity occurring in the presence of both he and his mother. In substance, Dana Garner's mother denies her presence in the area of the crimes on June 25, 1990, and she refutes several of Dana Garner's reasons for her presence at that time. In addition, several other members of his family claimed that Dana Garner's reputation for truthfulness was minimal.

At the trial of Rubin Ortega, the identification of Ortega as a principal in the homicide was given by two witnesses, (one being Dana Garner), and thus the evidence did not rest exclusively upon his testimony. We are unaware of any recantation by Garner to the June 25, 1990 shooting, and the totality of information does suggest that Garner was, in fact, present in New York on this date.

This information is provided to you for whatever course of action you deem appropriate.

Sincerely,

/ s /

Jon Besunder

Executive ADA

Homicide Bureau

Cc: Pamela M. Hirschhorn, Esq.

Rubin Ortega

Meanwhile, Garner had also been one of two witnesses to finger Rubin Ortega for a fatal shooting on June 25, 1990. On February 14, 1991, Ortega was convicted of murder in the second degree and criminal possession of a weapon in the second degree. Three weeks later he was sentenced to consecutive sentences of twenty-five years to life and five to fifteen years. Ortega's conviction was affirmed by the Appellate Division, Second Department, and permission to appeal to the Court of Appeals was denied in 1995.

On December 7, 1998, however, the Kings County DA's office wrote to Ortega's lawyer of record, alerting him to Blake's exoneration. Although the cases seemingly were not related, the DA's letter noted that Garner had testified he'd witnessed Blake murder two men on June 18, 1990. The carefully worded letter added: "Dana Garner was not present in New York City on June 18, 1990, and, therefore, . . . he did not see the events about which he testified." Executive ADA Jon Besunder also stated that questions had arisen about the truthfulness of Garner's testimony against Ortega as well, and he specified what some of them entailed. However, he concluded that "the totality of information does *suggest* [emphasis added] that Garner was, in fact, present in New York" on the date of Ortega's alleged murders. Besunder did not mention Garner's role in convicting Crosby.

In response to Besunder's letter, a postconviction motion was filed in 1999, but it was denied on the merits after a hearing in January 2000. A motion for permission to appeal was denied by the Appellate Division in an order published July 3, 2000. No further appeal of a postconviction motion is permitted under New York Criminal Procedure, and the standard of review in a federal habeas action is very high. Once the state court ruled against him, his chances of winning at the federal level would not be good.

In an affidavit and an interview with Dan Rather on CBS's *60 Minutes,* Garner recanted his testimony against Ortega as well as Blake and Crosby and claimed that the police had spoon-fed him details about Ortega's alleged crime.

Ortega's new appeals attorney, Steven Wasserman of the Legal Aid Society, continued to try to get his client a new trial. "The DA's letter should have been written five years earlier," Wasserman says. "Everybody knew then that Garner was a liar."

Wasserman filed a memorandum in support of Ortega's petition for a federal writ of habeas corpus. In it he claimed the trial court denied Ortega due process of law at his postconviction hearing. Wasserman said Garner claimed to have witnessed Blake commit a murder. A week later, Garner claimed he saw Ortega (his regular handball partner) commit murder.

"Both complaints were made the same day to the same detective," Wasserman said. "The two cases were supervised by the same sergeant, and both were presented to the grand jury on the same day. You tell me they're not linked!"

According to Wasserman, "There is no physical evidence, no circumstantial evidence, and no post-arrest statement that links Petitioner to the murder. . . . One of the two survivors, Angel Narvaez, testified

Steve Wasserman. *Author's photo.*

that Petitioner was not the person who shot him or Lionel Diaz. The other survivor, Ricardo Betances, initially disclaimed any ability to identify the perpetrator but eventually identified Petitioner after being shown his arrest photo by the same detective who obtained Garner's bogus complaint."

In repudiating his story that he witnessed Ortega commit the crime, Garner said he was pressured by police in the Seventy-fifth Precinct to level accusations against both Blake and Ortega. The police officers he named include Detective Richard Brew and supervising sergeant Michael Race, who was then overseeing the investigation of both homicides.

In March 2001, Garner testified that Blake's and Ortega's names were first raised by Detective Race, who also kept feeding him detailed information about the crimes. Garner also claimed Race and Brew were the officers involved in investigating his 1988 kidnapping that included the false testimony against Crosby. Both officers denied this.

In September 2001, District Judge John Gleeson of the Eastern District denied the federal habeas certificate and the certificate of appealability, saying that Ortega had failed to prove by a preponderance of the evidence that Garner's recantation was valid. He also rejected any claims of police or prosecutorial misconduct as "entirely unfounded."

On June 16, 2003, the U.S. Court of Appeals, Second Circuit, threw out Ortega's conviction and ordered a new trial—something that should have happened more than four years earlier. At this writing, the DA was deciding whether to retry the case.

Kings County

Detective Sergeant Michael Race

Detective Sergeant Michael Race worked in the Seventy-fifth Precinct's homicide squad in Brooklyn's East New York from December 1985 until his retirement in February 1993—a period of record-high murders. After leaving the New York Police Department (NYPD), he became a private investigator on Long Island, handling, among other cases, several alleged wrongful convictions.

In 1999 former police detective Sgt. Race came under criticism for his handling of the faulty murder case against Jeffrey Blake. But he also won praise, two years later, when as a private eye he helped defense attorney Ron Kuby win the exoneration of two men who had served fourteen years for killing a cab driver in Kings County. Working *pro bono*, Race had unearthed evidence pointing to another suspect. When the two men were freed, Race later confided to reporter Jim Dwyer of the *New York Times*, that he had handled 750 murder cases, only one of which was "done the correct way, from A to Z."

Detective Michael Race.
Courtesy of Bastienne Schmidt, New York magazine.

In response to the embarrassing publicity, instead of looking into wrongful arrests and convictions, the NYPD said it was investigating eighty suspicious murder cases Sgt. Race handled in East New York from 1989 to 1991, trying to determine if he improperly closed them without an arrest by blaming them on dead persons, thereby allowing the killers to go free. Rubin Ortega's defense lawyer, Steve Wasserman, said the department might better look into hundreds of Race's homicide cases (like Jeffrey Blake's and Rubin Ortega's) that had resulted in convictions—convictions that might bear special scrutiny.

Seeking Justice

For

Anthony Faison

URL/Web Page:
http://afaison.homestead.com/SeekingJustice.html
OR
http://geocities.com/shan22666/

Email: Faison2000@onebox.com

Voice Mail: 917 421-3902 X1527

Fax: 917 421-3902 X1527

Log on and join the fight to free him

Courtesy of Anthony Faison.

Michael S. Race

PRIVATE INVESTIGATOR

"Specialist in Criminal Matters"

(516) 409-0404

3941 Sunset Avenue, Seaford, New York 11783

Licensed and Bonded
Criminal and Civil

February 4, 1999

Mr. Anthony Faison 88 - A - 6157
Green Haven Correctional Facility
Route 216 Drawer "B"
Stormville, New York 12582-0010

Dear Mr. Faison,

I received all of the material that you had sent to me and I was quite impressed by reading all of it.

Now, as far as the criminal record of Carolyn Vanburen, the cost will be $100.00. If you gave a family member send me a money order in that amount, I will send the records to you upon receipt. That is all this case will cost you.

What I really want from you is the following information:
    Her: DD5 interview
        Grand Jury transcript
        Trial transcript
        DA's synopsis sheet
        Autopsy report

Once I track her down and interview her, I want to confront her with all of the evidence versus her testimony. I am sure that if you ask around, there is no problem with me obtaining sworn affidavits from witnesses. It is how it is presented and they all speak to me.

I will do this whole case for free. Like I had stated in the first paragraph, just the criminal record check will have a fee. Let me know what you would like to do and let's get started. Awaiting your reply.

Respectfully,

Michael S. Race

Courtesy of Anthony Faison.

Kings

"There Was Evidence Years Ago That These Young Men Were Innocent"

On March 14, 1987, police discovered livery driver Jean Ulysses shot to death in his cab in Brooklyn. A supposed bystander, Carolyn Van Buren, said she had been out drinking all night and witnessed the crime. She identified three men as taking part. Based on her testimony, two of them, Anthony Faison and Charles Shepard, were convicted of second-degree murder and sentenced to twenty-five years to life and fifteen years to life, respectively.

"It was like a real tremendous shock to me," Shepard later said. "I couldn't believe they said I was guilty of murder, for something I didn't do."

Both men continued to protest their innocence from prison. Faison sent more than sixty thousand letters and got friends to set up a Web site. One of his pleas reached Michael Race, the former veteran NYPD homicide detective turned private investigator, who decided to look into the case at his own expense.

A few months later, Race helped lawyers present new evidence that was used in a motion to set aside the conviction. But despite proof that the key eyewitness against the pair was a crack addict who had made up her story to collect a $1,000 reward, the Kings County DA refused to budge, and Supreme Court Justice Robert S. Kreindler denied the motion.

Working with high-profile radical lawyer Ron Kuby, Race dug up information that pinned the murder on Arlet Cheston and two others. A witness admitted he had helped Van Buren to wrongly identify Faison and Shepard. Fingerprint evidence from the crime scene was linked to Cheston. Faison and Shepard passed polygraph exams denying any involvement. And one of the jurors who had convicted Faison and Shepard said she had concluded they were not guilty but ultimately changed her vote in order to avoid having to be sequestered overnight in a motel.

SUPREME COURT STATE OF NEW YORK
COUNTY OF KINGS, CRIMINAL TERM
_____X

PEOPLE OF THE STATE OF NEW YORK   **AFFIDAVIT**
                   IND#5357 - 87

  ~against~

ANTHOINY FAISON and CHARLES SHEPARD

       Defendants
_____X

  I, **HELEN L. LILLEY**, residing at 1576 East 98th Street, Brooklyn New York, while

over the age of eighteen and being duly sworn, deposes and says that:

  I was a sworn juror in the homicide trial of Anthony Faison and Charles Shepard that

was held before the Hon. Robert Kreindler in Part 22 of Kings County Supreme Court.

  On the first day of jury deliberations, a vote was cast and there was one young

female black juror who stated that "she going to hold out and she didn't think that they

were guilty." When this young female black juror was informed that the jury was going

to be sequestered over night in a hotel, she then stated "that I can't stay" and then changed

her vote to guilty. The jury then found both of these defendants guilty and we then went

home without ever being sequestered.

             Helen Lilley
             Helen L. Lilley

Sworn to and subscribed in my
presence this _10_ day of
April 2001.

Michael S. Race

Michael S. Race

Deposition. *Courtesy of Ron Kuby.*

SUPREME COURT OF THE STATE OF NEW YORK
KINGS COUNTY: CRIMINAL TERM PART 7

--x

THE PEOPLE OF THE STATE OF NEW YORK,

    -against-   Ind. No. 5357/87

ANTHONY FAISON and
CHARLES SHEPARD,

           Defendants.
--x

MEMORANDUM OF LAW IN SUPPORT OF DEFENDANTS' MOTION TO VACATE JUDGMENT ON THE BASIS OF NEWLY-DISCOVERED EVIDENCE, PURSUANT TO N.Y.C.P.L. §440.10

Ronald L. Kuby
740 Broadway, 5th floor
New York, NY 10003
(212) 529-0223

Dated: New York, New York
       April 30, 2001

440 Motion. *Courtesy of Ron Kuby.*

SUPREME COURT OF THE STATE OF NEW YORK
KINGS COUNTY: CRIMINAL TERM PART 7

--x

THE PEOPLE OF THE STATE OF NEW YORK,

    -against-   Ind. No. 5357/87

ANTHONY FAISON and
CHARLES SHEPARD,

          Defendants.

--x

MEMORANDUM OF LAW IN SUPPORT OF DEFENDANTS' MOTION TO
VACATE JUDGMENT ON THE BASIS OF NEWLY-DISCOVERED EVIDENCE,
PURSUANT TO N.Y.C.P.L. §440.10.

INTRODUCTION

    This case once again forces this Court to confront one
of the worst nightmares of the criminal justice system; two
men confined to life in prison for a murder they did not
commit, while the actual killers walk free.

    In the fourteen years that Anthony Faison and Charles
Shepard have been incarcerated for the murder of Jean
Ulysses, they have consistently and passionately maintained
their innocence. Their case, and the persistent questions
surrounding their guilt, have caught the attention of local
and national media. Since 1999, Michael S. Race, a former
Detective Sergeant in charge of the 75th Detective Squad
Homicide Unit who has since become a private investigator,
has worked pro bono to clear their names. Mr. Race has not

1

Excerpt from brief. *Courtesy of Ron Kuby.*

On May 14, 2001, Justice Kreindler scheduled another hearing to consider Kuby's motions. Faison hoped he would soon be free. But, at the hearing, Kreindler pressed prosecutors to explain why Faison and Shepard should be exonerated. "I presided at the trial in '87 and, very frankly, after hearing the testimony I was pretty well convinced both defendants were guilty," Kreindler said. "It's hard to believe that a person for a rather small reward would name two innocent people as murderers." Finally, he reversed the conviction and ordered the two prisoners freed. They had spent more than thirteen years wrongly imprisoned.

In filing a $60 million lawsuit for wrongful conviction, Kuby said, "There was ample evidence years ago that these young men were innocent and that the sole witness against them was lying—and the district attorney's office adamantly refused to reopen the case."

Queens

"God Will Look into This"

In 1979 a ten-year-old boy told police he'd seen a neighborhood man throw a two-year-old child off the roof of a three-story building onto the concrete. (The child miraculously survived.) Based on the eyewitness account, Charles Daniels was convicted of attempted second-degree murder and first-degree sodomy.

At the time of the crime, Daniels was employed and had never been arrested, and acquaintances attested to his good character. Suddenly sentenced to six to eighteen years in prison, he was branded a "baby raper" and subjected to horrible physical abuse and harassment by corrections staff and inmates, who beat him, urinated in his food, and set his cell mattress on fire.

But after the intervention of Alan Axelrod and William Hellerstein of the Legal Aid Society, on August 18, 1982, the Appellate Division, Second Department, reversed the conviction and remanded the case to supreme court in Queens for a new trial, citing the trial court's defective instruction to the jury about alibi and eyewitness identification. The

Rooftop crime scene. *Courtesy of Lawrence Halford.*

fifteen-page opinion also criticized defense counsel, Kenneth R. Bruce, for "woefully inadequate and grossly insufficient" legal representation.

The landmark opinion in *People v. Daniels* was written by none other than Justice Frank D. O'Connor, who, thirty years earlier, had served as the defense attorney in the case of mistaken eyewitness identification that provided the basis for Alfred Hitchcock's classic film *The Wrong Man.*

Hellerstein and Larry Halfond of the Legal Aid Society dug deeper into Daniels's case with a seasoned investigator, Ed Perrazzo, aided by news stories by legendary crime reporter Selwyn Raab that appeared in the *New York Times.* The probe ultimately exonerated Daniels and cast suspicion on the state's sole eyewitness. It turned out the youth in question had a record of psychological disturbance and sexual offenses against children.

Three months after the appellate court's ruling, Queens district attorney John Santucci dropped the charges. Freed at last from his four-year ordeal, Daniels expressed no anger for how he had been treated, saying only, "God will look into this."

Attorney Lawrence F. Spirn of Woodbury later helped gain Daniels an award of $600,000 based on his civil rights claim.

```
DATE    09-28-78              STATE OF NEW YORK          TRANS NO 1043;
TIME    1500         DIVISION OF CRIMINAL JUSTICE SERVICES  PAGE   1
FAX NO  0016298              ALBANY, NEW YORK  12203
RUN NO  9719                                               DOB    10-25-43
        CONFIDENTIAL  TO:    NYCPD HDQ                      RAC    NEGRO
                                                           SEX    MALE
                                                           HGT    5-10
I NAME  DANIELS,CHARLES                    I  I NYSID  4327960N I  SOC
                                                           FBI
                            NAMES USED BY SUBJECT
DANIELS,CHARLES


            < < < < < < CRIMINAL HISTORY > > > > > >
     ARREST INFORMATION              DISPO AND CORRECTION INFORMATION

09-27-78 NYCPD PCT 103
    COURT CONTROL NO  4042275N
    AGENCY ID NUMBER  10323435
    ARR PL    QUEENS COUNTY
    CRM PL    QUEENS COUNTY

ATT-PL   A FEL  HOMICIDE
    PL   B FEL  SODOMY
    PL   A MISD ENDANGER CHILD
            < < < < < < OTHER INFORMATION > > > > > >
I TYPE  I  DATE   I                    COMMENTS
3TH INFO|OCT  25,1943| FREQ 01                      NEW YORK   FREQ  01
NAME AND|SEPT 27,1978| DANIELS,CHARLES
ADDRESS |           |     109 30 160 ST        QUEENS        NEW YORK
```

Daniel's wrongful rap sheet. *Courtesy of Lawrence Halford.*

Lawrence Halford. *Author's photo.*

Overburdened defense lawyer Sean P. Sullivan in his office. *Courtesy of Ruth Fremson, The New York Times.*

4

Ineffective Counsel

Since the U.S. Supreme Court ruling of *Gideon v. Wainwright* (1963), New York and other states have been constitutionally required to provide counsel to all eligible persons in criminal proceedings. County Law Article 18-B mandates that each county allocate funds for the assignment of counsel to all indigent criminal defendants.

But New York's patchwork of public defense systems, which has never been adequately funded or regulated, often teeters on the brink of collapse. In 2000 a series by *The New York Times* reported that in New York City the number of lawyers representing indigent defendants had dropped to twelve hundred, from twenty-two hundred in 1993, and it attributed the decline to the fact that New York State paid defense lawyers for the poor at rates that were the second lowest in the nation: only $40 an hour for in-court work and $25 an hour for out-of-court work. One attorney for the indigent who was featured in the series (Sean P. Sullivan) had a criminal caseload of sixteen hundred clients, no secretary, and no filing system. Such problems are bound to deny many defendants effective counsel, thereby contributing to innumerable injustices, including many wrongful convictions.

Some public defenders manage to provide excellent representation, at trial or postconviction, and bad lawyering can also occur among private counsel. But poor people lack the ability to shop around for the best lawyers that money can buy, and their defenders don't enjoy the resources of strong investigative support and other help. Many indigent defendants consider prosecutors and public defenders to be much too cozy with each other.

Ineffective assistance of counsel at trial and on direct appeal violates the Sixth Amendment right to a fair trial. But proving it is extremely difficult. The U.S. Supreme Court, in *Strickland v. Washington*, established a standard that is "highly deferential" to the performance of counsel. Thus, to succeed with a claim of ineffective assistance of counsel, a defendant must overcome "a strong presumption that counsel's conduct falls within the wide range of professional assistance," show that counsel's performance "fell below an objective standard of reasonableness," and establish "prejudice"—which is defined as a "reasonable possibility that counsel's errors affected the outcome." Because this is such a remarkably low standard, courts are reluctant to find such fault, even when the lawyer's conduct was atrocious. From 1984 to 2000, the nation's highest court never found a single instance of ineffective assistance of counsel.

Yet ineffective assistance of counsel greatly contributes to many wrongful convictions, especially because negligent representation by defense counsel allows many other kinds of errors, such as mistaken identification and eyewitness perjury, to occur unchallenged. Although the claim rarely succeeds, it offers appeals lawyers a gateway to bring up other issues, such as the trial lawyer's failure to examine juror misconduct, the government's obligation to turn over exculpatory evidence, and a host of other flaws.

New York

Inexplicable Nonfeasance of Counsel

Efren Meralla was charged with a murder as part of a double homicide that was committed in New York in 1987. He was represented by retained counsel and acquitted.

But Meralla was later charged with another defendant for the other murder. The same prosecutor presented essentially the same circumstantial case. But by the second trial, Meralla had become indigent, and he was represented by an Article 18-B attorney. This time he was convicted and sentenced to twenty-five years to life.

Appellate counsel challenged the conviction based on trial counsel's failure to make pretrial motions for a severance and for the exclusion of evidence on which the defendant had already been acquitted. But in 1994, Supreme Court Justice Dorothy Cropper denied appellant's motions.

Joanne Legano Ross of the Legal Aid Society appealed to the Appellate Division. On June 4, 1996, the Appellate Division, First Department, unanimously reversed the conviction, finding the defendant was denied effective assistance of counsel at his second trial. The court ruled that "the inexplicable nonfeasance of counsel amounted to fundamentally flawed, less than meaningful representation," and found that "counsel's purported strategy . . . was not only flawed but poorly executed, resulting in unfair prejudice which substantially impaired the defense."

In 1998, Justice Michael J. Obus dismissed the indictment and Meralla was freed.

Onondaga

A Stiff Standard

After his 1989 conviction in Onondaga County for sexually assaulting his two young sons during a divorce dispute, Kenneth G. Pavel fought to prove his innocence. Although paroled in 1998, Pavel had continued to refuse to admit guilt, insisting that he was innocent. As a result, he'd been sent back to prison as a parole violator.

In July 2001 the U.S. Court of Appeals for the Second Circuit ordered him released from prison, finding that Pavel had been denied effective representation by his trial defense attorney "in three distinct ways." The court said his trial attorney failed to prepare an adequate defense because he thought the charges would be dismissed; also, he should have called fact witnesses and medical experts. Although the court was reluctant to question the lawyer's strategic decisions, it commended Pavel's appellate attorneys for "providing their client with superbly effective assistance of counsel" on his appeal for eight years, without compensation.

James V. Gara, of Kelley Drye & Warren LLP in New York City, who represented Pavel in his habeas petition, noted the difficulty of winning on grounds of ineffective counsel. "We had to demonstrate that this was not just a failed strategy, and that is a pretty stiff standard," he told the *New York Law Journal*. The district attorney later decided not to continue prosecution.

Interviewed for this book, Gara remarked, "My experience with this case convinced me, never get charged with a crime north of White Plains, because they don't need any evidence to convict."

Another interviewee—former veteran Parole Board commissioner Anthony K. Umina—confided that, based on his study of the case, he was convinced that Pavel had been wrongfully convicted. "It always bothered me," he said.

Queens

The Importance of Packaging

In October 1993, two crime victims identified a former acquaintance as the man who had carried out a terrifying push-in robbery of their home in Laurelton, Queens. The suspect denied the charge and offered an alibi, saying he had flown to North Carolina with his girlfriend shortly before the robbery occurred. He even produced a ticket stub and photographs of himself with friends down south during the weekend in question.

But Arthur Stewart, age twenty-four, an African American male with a history of drug and weapon charges, had little money. When he could no longer afford to pay his privately retained counsel, he had to settle for a court-appointed attorney from the 18-B panel.

The airline ticket alibi. *Courtesy of Wilmer Cutler and Pickering.*

That lawyer failed to introduce some crucial evidence, including corroborative testimony by a USAir flight attendant, on Stewart's behalf. The jury deadlocked and later acquitted Stewart on the robbery counts. But he was convicted of first-degree burglary and second-degree robbery. Judge Sheri S. Roman sentenced him to seven to fourteen years in prison.

After appeals based on claims of ineffective counsel failed to convince the Appellate Division, Second Department, and the Court of Appeals, Stewart seemed likely to serve out the rest of his sentence in state prison.

But in early 1999, the prisoner took matters into his own hands and filed a *pro se* writ of federal habeas corpus that ended up on the desk of Eastern District judge Edward R. Korman. Something about it prompted the judge to respond. Korman, a former state prosecutor, appointed two lawyers from a top corporate law firm to represent the prisoner in his action, and the attorneys—Lewis J. Liman and Gayton P. Gomez of Wilmer, Cutler and Pickering—responded by spending more than three hundred hours reviewing the case.

"From the start I began to see that Stewart had been the victim of inadequate counsel and that he was innocent," Gomez says. "The police had really screwed up on the night of the crime. But the habeas standards that exist today are insane, so that our best bet was to try to get a new trial. Our best witness—the flight attendant—was now dead, and in fact, the only evidence that I had in hand was really the same evidence that had been used to convict my client in the first place. The best we could do was to repackage the evidence for presentation to the Queens district attorney."

Gomez's well-tooled brief prompted the DA's Appeals Bureau to take a second look at the case, and it was assigned to a team headed by Deputy Executive Assistant District Attorney Charles A. Testagrossa, who gave it special attention. Testagrossa offered Stewart and his former girlfriend an opportunity to take a polygraph test.

In late June 2001, Gomez received a telephone call from the DA's office. "Before I knew it, he said they planned to dismiss the indictment, ask the judge to vacate the conviction, and get Stewart released from prison. It was exciting." But Gomez adds, "What changed in those six years?—only that there were some different individuals involved. And all the resources of a major law firm. And we got lucky. It went to the right person in the DA's office. But, really, the evidence was still the same as that which convicted him."

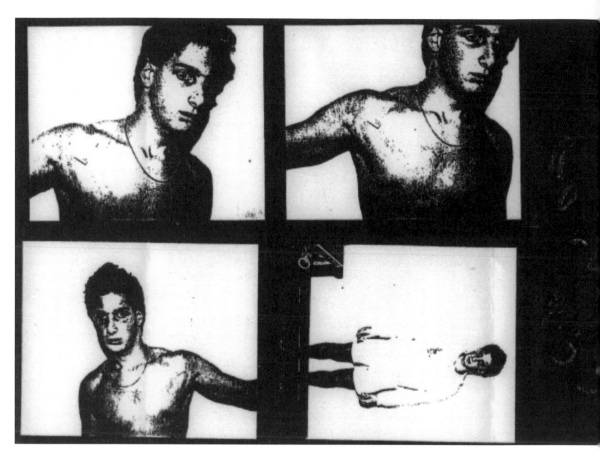

Martin Tankleff in the Suffolk Police interrogation room.
Courtesy of Martin Tankleff.

5

False Confessions

A confession is considered one of the strongest forms of evidence of guilt in criminal law—so much so that it can dominate everything else presented at trial. For that reason, police and prosecutors have always done everything they can to get the suspect to admit his guilt.

For decades, police officers in New York and throughout the United States routinely used brute force to obtain confessions and guilty pleas. In the 1880s, Captain Cornelius Williams of the New York Police Department explained how officers were trained to beat suspects into admitting guilt, so the criminal didn't "beat the charges." Near the start of the twentieth century, Inspector Thomas Byrnes, the commander of all NYPD detectives, referred to such systematic, illegal coercion of suspects as the "third degree." Police often held suspects incommunicado and subjected them to forms of physical torture to get an admission. Although such extortionist practices were widely known to everyone, little was done to stop them, and they continued behind closed doors. The torturers were taught how to beat someone without leaving marks.

In 1931 a panel chaired by a prominent New York lawyer and former U.S. attorney general, George Wickersham, undertook the first federal assessment of law enforcement in the United States. During the heated commission hearings, Buffalo's police chief and other law enforcement leaders openly expressed contempt for constitutional rights protecting individual suspects. The Wickersham Commission's massive report documented the widespread use of the third degree, fabrication of evidence, coercion of witnesses, bribery, entrapment, and illegal arrests. It defined the third degree as "the inflicting of pain, physical or mental, to extract confessions or statements."

Spurred in part by many years of such disclosures, the U.S. Supreme Court gradually expanded the concept of "voluntariness" in confessions and guilty pleas through rulings such as *Miranda v. Arizona* (1966), which specifically referenced abuses in New York. In the face of many new legal requirements protecting the rights of criminal suspects, police and prosecutors continued to become more sophisticated in their interrogation techniques and plea-bargaining methods. Gradually the emphasis became more psychological than physical.

By 2000, one legal authority on New York police abuses, Professor Paul Chevigny of New York University Law School, observed that the "minimization of the use of coerced confessions and the decrease in police use of deadly force" had become "among the success stories of human rights in the United States."

At the same time, by most accounts, allegations of "false confessions" also diminished from their pre-*Miranda* levels. The incidence of false confessions has not ended, however, and some scholars, such as Professor Richard Leo of the University of California at Irvine, continue to document alleged instances in which questionable confessions were obtained by suspicious means. Some defendants still allege that their confessions (or guilty pleas) were coerced and involuntary, resulting in their own wrongful conviction.

Monroe

The People v. Betty Tyson and John Duval

In 1973 the body of a murdered white Kodak consultant was found in the red-light district of downtown Rochester, a company town, and the police were under intense pressure to find the killer. Three days later, detectives arrested two local black known prostitutes, Betty Tyson, a

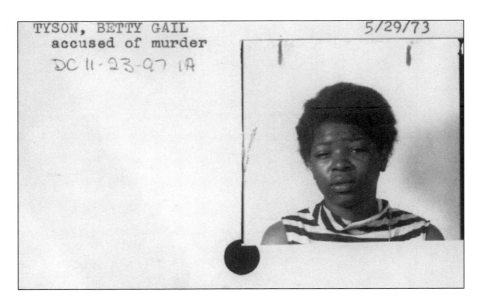

TYSON, BETTY GAIL   5/29/73
accused of murder
DC 11-23-97 1A

Betty Tyson shortly after her arrest.
Courtesy of the Rochester Democrat and Chronicle.

heroin addict, and John Duval, a transvestite, claiming the pair had confessed to robbing and murdering the victim during a sexual encounter.

At trial, defense attorneys pointed out the lack of physical evidence and challenged the confessions. Tyson claimed she had been handcuffed to a chair and beaten; Duval said he had been worked over after initially refusing to agree to a statement. They alleged that after twelve hours of the third degree, they had finally signed a bogus confession that had been concocted by the notorious lead police detective, William Mahoney. But the prosecution brought forward two other prostitutes who testified they had seen Tyson and Duval with the victim the night of the murder, and one of them said that Duval had described the killing to them. When all was said and done, Tyson and Duval were convicted by an all-white jury and sentenced to twenty-five years to life.

After Tyson and Duval had spent more than six years in prison, a local newspaper reporter and some appeals lawyers began to look into the case more closely.

Detective Mahoney was investigated for brutality and receiving favors from mobsters, but he managed to escape punishment until 1980,

Detective William Mahoney. *Courtesy of the Rochester Democrat and Chronicle.*

when a federal grand jury convicted him of fabricating evidence in another murder case. Gerald Houlihan, the U.S. attorney who successfully prosecuted him, later told the Rochester *Democrat and Chronicle*, "I don't believe that Bill Mahoney was corrupt in the sense that he made up evidence against people he thought were innocent. He was corrupt in that he corrupted the criminal justice system." But the newspaper also reported that Mahoney had been infamous for his ability to get confessions, sometimes after yanking suspects by the hair, smashing them with telephone books, or burning them with lighted cigarettes. One of his nicknames was "Backroom Bill."

Tyson's mother said she had inspected her daughter's injuries at the jail and asked Betty's previous attorney to photograph them, but he'd failed to do so. Later the defense discovered that two counselors at the jail had also met with Tyson in custody at the facility shortly after her arrest. They said she was covered with welts and bruises and had told them she'd been severely beaten by police. In fact, when the two staffers had told this to jail authorities, they'd been forced to leave the institution and their program was shut down. The defense had never been informed.

New information also emerged about the two prostitutes who had testified for the prosecution at the trial. It turned out that although they claimed not to know anything about the killing, they had been ordered held in jail as material witnesses. One of them now confided he had spent seven months in confinement, much of it in solitary, during which time the police told him what to say and warned him he would go to prison for perjury if he told the truth. He said one night he awoke to find Detective Mahoney sitting nearby, spinning the cylinder of his revolver and threatening him if he didn't cooperate.

When the defense team gained access to the original police file, they learned that the other key witness had actually stated that he'd never seen Tyson with anyone resembling the victim—exactly the opposite of what had been presented at the trial. Yet this document had never been shared with the defense.

The defense lawyers found themselves up against some important figures in the local legal establishment. The assistant district attorney

Betty Tyson leaving jail with her lawyer, John Getz. *Courtesy of John Getz.*

who had prosecuted Tyson, Ray Cornelius, had become a state supreme court judge. Another ADA at the time, Howard Relin, was now district attorney. Getting past them and their cronies would not be easy.

As of 1998, Tyson and Duval remained in prison. Having spent more than twenty-five years in confinement, Tyson was the state's longest-serving female inmate. On May 21 of that year she was planting collards and string beans in the prison garden when a guard summoned her to see the warden. Bedford Hills superintendent Elaine Lord informed her that a judge had just overturned her conviction. Monroe County judge John J. Connell had ruled that the city police illegally withheld evidence that could have helped prove her innocence, and he called the conviction "a travesty of justice." Inmates cheered.

But a week later, District Attorney Relin offered no apology. In announcing his decision not to retry Tyson, Relin said, "Ms. Tyson has already served 25 years in the state prison system. That means that, even if we were to retry her again and be successful in a second prose-cution, that she would be immediately eligible for parole. Six witnesses from the original trial have died in the intervening 25-plus years; and several of those witnesses are critical to the statement that was allegedly made. Also, it would cost our office thousands of dollars and it would cost the taxpayers of Monroe County thousands of dollars to resuscitate this case."

In November 1998, however, the City of Rochester settled out of court with Tyson. As part of the agreement, the city paid her $1.25 mil-lion, and Mayor William A. Johnson Jr.—a former director of the Urban League of Rochester, who had supported her unsuccessful bid for guber-natorial clemency in 1988—issued a formal apology.

The question then was what would happen to Duval. Although he'd twice told the Parole Board that he had committed the murder, Duval now said he had done so only to express remorse in order to enhance his chances of release. A Monroe County judge overturned Duval's murder conviction on the same grounds that were cited in Tyson's case. This time, Relin proceeded with a retrial, but Duval was ultimately acquitted. He later filed suit against the state for $100 million.

Reporter Gary Craig

The freeing of Betty Tyson in 1998 drew national attention to an investigative reporter for the Rochester *Democrat and Chronicle*, Gary Craig, whose years of relentless stories about the case helped persuade the powers-that-be to reverse her conviction and drop further prosecution. Craig's reporting drew glowing profiles in the *New York Times* and *Brill's Content*. But as the *Brill's* piece made clear, the reporter's toughest obstacle was not the legal system—it was his own newspaper's editors, whose job it was to rake him over the coals until they were convinced he was right.

"They Ask You to Prove a Negative"

Court of Claims Judge Donald Corbett Jr. (of Rochester) ruled that the existing state law didn't allow Betty Tyson to seek compensation. The reason he cited was that a judge had reversed her conviction because the police had withheld evidence that could have proven her innocence, and then the prosecution had decided not to retry her—meaning that she hadn't demonstrated her innocence at trial, as required by statute. According to his interpretation, Tyson might have qualified for an award if she had been retried and acquitted, but because the DA had decided not to proceed, she didn't meet the statutory test. "Unfortunately for Betty Tyson, there can be no recovery here, and no opportunity for her to prove her innocence, perhaps her ultimate goal," Judge Corbett said in his decision.

In June 2001 the Court of Appeals declined to review a decision of the Appellate Division, Fourth Department, thus upholding the dismissal of Tyson's $12.5 million wrongful imprisonment lawsuit in the New York State Court of Claims.

Tyson's attorney, Jon Getz, says, "The courts are not concerned about innocence. It's not their thing. Yet the way the unjust convictions law is drafted, they force you to prove a negative, making you prove you were not guilty—that you were adjudged innocent." Getz adds, "No county court judge is going to write an opinion saying he's

Reporter Gary Craig. *Courtesy of Gary Craig.*

reversing a conviction because the person was innocent. The way that convictions are typically overturned and people are released has nothing to do with innocence; rather, it involves unconstitutional things, statutory violations. Yet the Court of Claims demands that you prove your client was found innocent at trial and suffered injury as a result."

The Leyra Case. From Erik Barnow, *Media Marathon:
A Twentieth-Century Memoir.* © 1996. *Courtesy of Duke Univesity Press.*

Kings

Hypnotically Induced Confession

On January 11, 1950, the front page of the *Daily News* carried a grue-some crime scene photo beneath the headline "FIND AGED PAIR HACKED TO DEATH."

In the murders' wake, teams of Brooklyn police questioned the vic-tims' fifty-year-old son, Camilo "Bud" Leyra, for three days and nights, allowing him only a half-hour of sleep. After Leyra complained of unbearable sinus pains, they brought in a doctor. Unbeknownst to Leyra, however, the physician turned out to be a psychiatrist trained in hypno-tism, whom the police had offered to pay a bonus if he extracted a confes-sion. The psychiatrist put his hand on Leyra's forehead and went to work, eliciting responses that were secretly tape-recorded. Based on these utter-ances, three different juries in Brooklyn later convicted Leyra of the dou-ble murder, and three times he was sentenced to die in the electric chair.

Frederick M. Scholem had been Leyra's court-appointed lawyer, but in those days the state's support of indigent clients did not include appeals. Yet Scholem persisted at his own expense because he was convinced of his client's innocence. Working with renowned *pro bono* advocate Osmond K. Fraenkel, Schloem built a strong case against the confession.

Leyra spent five years awaiting execution at Sing Sing, some of it within earshot of Julius and Ethel Rosenberg, the condemned atomic spies. Finally a judge set Leyra free, based on issues of "fair procedure" centering on his incriminating statements to the psychiatrist.

Leyra's case was the subject of an award-winning documentary film, *The Constitution and Fair Procedures*, that appeared on national television in the late 1950s.

Getting Leyra's Confession

From *People v. Leyra*, 302i N.Y. 353, 99 N.E.2d 553, 556–557 (1951)

Captain Meenahan, at about 7:00 P.M. on that evening, introduced defendant to a physician, who is also a specialist in neurology and psychiatry, a psychologist, and one who uses the technique of psycho-analysis in his practice. The doctor, unconnected with the police department or the prosecutor's office, had been called to the police station by the District Attorney, who outlined the case to him. The doctor had also been "briefed" by Captain Meenahan, as is manifest from the questions he asked. He agreed to talk to defendant upon condition that there be no one else in the room; he knew, however, that the room was wired and that the interview would be electrically recorded by a recording machine, which was typically set up that day. The police and the District Attorney were in the basement of the police station, where they overheard the entire interview and permitted it to continue uninterruptedly. The doctor spent an hour or an hour and a half with defendant.

A transcript of the recorded interview shows that he told defendant at the outset: "I'll tell you what the purpose of my talk to you is. I want to see if I can help you." To this the defendant answered: "Yes, Doctor." The doctor asked him about his sinus condition and the treatment he had had, and in the course of the interview said: "I'm your doctor." The transcript further discloses that on at least forty occasions the doctor in one way or another promised to help defendant, and on one occasion said: "I know you are in a little trouble. We do sometimes things that are not right, but in a fit of anger we sometimes do things that we aren't really responsible for. I want to see whether or not you did something but which you've done in a fit of temper or anger. Do you understand me? A. Yes." . . .

After more conversation, the following took place:

Q. I want you to recollect and tell me everything. I am going to make you remember and recollect back and bring back thoughts—thoughts which you think you might have forgotten. I can make you recollect them. It's entirely to your benefit to recollect them because, you see, you're a nervous boy. You got irritable and you might have got in a fit of temper. Tell me, I am here to help you. A. I wish you could, Doctor.

Q. I am going to put my hand on your forehead and as I put my hand on your forehead you are going to bring back all these thoughts that are coming to your mind. I am going to keep my hand on your forehead and I am going to ask you questions and now you will be able to tell me.

Kings

Whitmore: The Case That Shook New York

On August 28, 1963—the day of Martin Luther King's historic Freedom March on Washington—the mutilated bodies of two young "career girls" were found in their Upper East Side apartment. Janice Wylie, the daughter of a well-known author, and Emily Hoffert, the child of a prominent surgeon, had been horribly raped and murdered, setting off a high-profile hunt for the killer or killers.

Seven months later, a slender nineteen-year-old Negro youth, George Whitmore Jr., was being questioned about an attempted rape and robbery in Brooklyn when police discovered in his wallet a snapshot of two white girls who appeared to resemble Wylie and Hoffert. This set off a frenzy of interrogation by teams of police and prosecutors from Brooklyn and Manhattan. When it was over, Whitmore was arrested for the attempted rape and robbery. He was also accused of the Wylie-Hoffert slayings.

 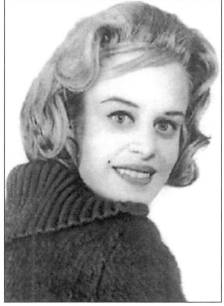

Emily Hoffert (*left*) and Janice Wylie. *New York Police Department.*

Chief of Detectives Lawrence J. McKearney told the press, "We got the right guy—no question about it. He gave us details only the killer could know." Brooklyn prosecutors hailed Whitmore's sixty-one-page statement the most detailed confession in the city's history.

Coming less than two weeks after another killer, Eddie Lee Mays, was executed in Sing Sing, Whitmore's case seemed to have death penalty written all over it.

After the court appointed inexperienced counsel to represent him, Whitmore told his lawyer the police had forced him to confess to a crime he knew nothing about. But the attorney put up a weak defense. A Brooklyn jury quickly convicted the youth of attempted rape and assault, and the judge sentenced him to an indeterminate term of up to life imprisonment—and that was just the beginning. Facing an even grimmer prospect on the Manhattan murder charges, Whitmore's family managed to obtain the services of two veteran lawyers, Arthur H. Miller and Stanley J. Reiben.

Reporters, including Selwyn Raab, then of the *World-Telegram and The Sun,* began to look into the case and immediately became suspicious of the official version. Whitmore's alibi seemed solid. Other aspects of the case didn't add up. Raab started finding evidence of abuse. One of his stories revealed that a juror in the attempted rape case had made racial slurs against the youth.

But the biggest bombshell exploded in late January 1965, when Manhattan prosecutors suddenly charged an ex-convict with the Wylie-Hoffert slayings. Richard Robles, age twenty-three, a white heroin addict on parole for assault, was said to have admitted killing the women, and there appeared to be a lot of physical evidence against him.

As a result, Whitmore's "confession" immediately became suspect. Experts offered all kinds of theories to try to explain how the police might have obtained such a detailed but patently false account of a crime. Some writers speculated that the youth's "low intelligence" and desire to please male authority figures had made him particularly susceptible to police intimidation. But many observers simply concluded that unscrupulous police and prosecutors had coerced him into giving a false confession.

George Whitmore leaves Brooklyn court with his mother. *Courtesy of Corbis.*

Although Robles was convicted and sentenced to life for the Wylie-Hoffert murders, Whitmore's ordeal dragged on for years. Brooklyn supreme court justice David Malbin threw out Whitmore's conviction for the attempted rape and assault, due to the juror's prejudiced remarks. But the Kings County DA still went after him with a fury, getting him reconvicted and sentenced to five to ten years. Another trial for a different Brooklyn murder resulted in a hung jury, and those charges were eventually dropped. Released on bail, Whitmore continued to suffer police harassment.

The Appellate Division finally reversed Whitmore's conviction for attempted rape and assault and ordered a third trial, but after years of litigation, those charges, too, were finally dropped. Whitmore was finally free. But he and his family had suffered tremendously.

The police and prosecutors who had obtained Whitmore's bogus confession and hounded him for years eventually retired, without being held accountable for their actions.

But the Whitmore case had enormous ramifications in criminal justice for years to come. The U.S. Supreme Court, in *Miranda v. Arizona* (1966), referred to Whitmore in condemning backroom police interrogation practices. The episode also helped to lend support to a legislatively recommended moratorium on capital punishment. Whitmore's ordeal provided the basis for several books, including Raab's *Justice in the Back Room* (1967), and inspired a popular movie and the highly successful *Kojak* television series, marking it as a case that shook an entire system.

Selwyn Raab, Investigative Reporter

Over his long career, veteran investigative reporter Selwyn Raab has worked to free many wrongly accused persons, including Hurricane Carter. But his role in New York's landmark Whitmore case helped transform American criminal law, reform police procedures, and end capital punishment—at least for a while.

Raab's involvement in the Whitmore case started after some of his stories about police brutality so impressed one of Whitmore's fellow patients at Bellevue Hospital that he sent the reporter a daily diary that Whitmore had kept. As the reporter dug into the story, he determined that Whitmore could not have committed the Wylie-Hoffert murders, because he was in Wildwood, New Jersey, celebrating news broadcasts of the Freedom March. Raab also discovered that authorities had long known that the "suspicious" snapshot police had said linked Whitmore to the double slaying was really not suspicious at all—yet they had not revealed it. And he uncovered the fact that key evidence used to convict Whitmore of attempted rape was also bogus. (Police had said a button the victim had snatched from her assailant's coat matched Whitmore's missing button, but the FBI Crime Lab had confided that this wasn't true.) Raab's stories about the case exposed rampant police abuses, prosecutorial overzealousness and chicanery, judicial favoritism, uneven lawyering, and public bigotry.

"I knew the kid was innocent," Raab says. "Cops knew it, but said nothing. [Manhattan DA] Frank Hogan—supposedly such a legal giant—knew it too, but he also kept quiet. They were determined to convict him of something in order to prove they hadn't been totally wrong."

Finally, Raab and lawyer Michael Beldock flew to Puerto Rico to locate a missing witness, who discredited the account of the alleged victim of the attempted rape. When confronted with the truth, Brooklyn district attorney Eugene Gold had no choice but to drop the charges against Whitmore.

"In the end, it was publicity that saved George Whitmore," says Raab. "There was no Legal Aid Society then and a two-bit murder would have kept him in prison for life. But because it was such a high-profile crime, the truth came out."

Asked what might be done today to prevent wrongful convictions, Raab says, "Make the DA play fair."

"We Can't Have Criminals Getting Off on a Technicality"

Manhattan defense attorney Jack S. Hoffinger represented Richard Robles, the man convicted of the Wylie-Hoffert murders.

"Robles wasn't factually innocent, there really was no question about that," Hoffinger says. "But he'd been questioned without his lawyer being present. The issue was whether the confessions were voluntary, legitimate, and admissible. The Court of Appeals at the time said, in *People v. Robles*, by a vote of five to two, that they were. Five years later, in *People v. Hobson*, the Court reversed itself and ruled that that kind of behavior was not acceptable.

"Stanley Fuld was one of the judges on the Court that decided *Robles* and I knew him. When Fuld said, 'I'm not here to debate the facts in this case,' I knew where he was headed. It was, like, we can't have criminals getting off on a technicality. I said something like, 'The point is whether we have a Constitution that has to be lived up to, or don't we? Certainly there are totalitarian countries that do better against street crime than we do, but they don't have the Bill of Rights in those places.'

"He knew I was a former prosecutor and I said, 'I've been around long enough to accept the fact that the police violate the Constitution every day. But the Bill of Rights is there to impede the police—to make sure they don't have unbridled power. And prosecutors are not supposed to engage in violations of the Constitution.'

"I came out of the office of Frank Hogan—the office of the Manhattan district attorney—and I was taught that prosecutors are not cops. DAs are lawyers, who are supposed to *uphold* the Constitution. They take an oath to do that. For me the *Robles* case was a defining moment of how facts make law. *Robles* wasn't a matter of wrongful conviction on the facts—a case of factual innocence. But it was one in which so-called technical arguments—which means whether or not you're going to uphold the Constitution—carried the day."

Suffolk

Good Police Work or "False Confession"?

At 6:17 a.m. on September 17, 1988, Suffolk police arrived at a fashionable home in Belle Terre, Suffolk County, Long Island, in response to a frantic 911 call made by one of the residents, Martin H. Tankleff, who was barely seventeen years old. They found him outside the home, yelling that someone had murdered his parents. Inside the house they found Tankleff's adoptive mother lying dead in the master bedroom, and her husband unconscious and gravely wounded in the study. Both appeared to have been bludgeoned and stabbed.

Young Tankleff told police that when he awoke to get ready for school, he had discovered their bodies. He said he suspected his father's former business partner, Jerry Steuerman. (Investigation later revealed that Steuerman owed Seymour Tankleff a great deal of money—more than $350,000. On the night of the murder, he'd also played in a high-stakes poker game at Tankleff's house.)

A tag team of homicide detectives began interrogating the youth. Four hours later, one of them, Suffolk County police investigator K. James McCready, left the interrogation room and went to a nearby phone, where he could be overheard taking a call. When he returned,

Seymour and Arlene Tankleff, Martin Tankleff's
parents. *Courtesy of Martin Tankleff.*

McCready told Tankleff that his father had come out of a coma and
accused him of the crime. The youth was incredulous. After more
questioning, young Tankleff reportedly said, "I need psychiatric help."
Later he began to make incriminating statements, according to the
police.

As it turned out, McCready's story about the telephone call was
untrue—he had used it as a ruse to get the traumatized youth to confess.
But the police and prosecutors used the patently false statements to support formal charges of murder against Tankleff for the death of both his
parents, alleging that he had attacked them because they wouldn't buy
him a new car.

Martin Tankleff in prison. *Courtesy of Martin Tankleff.*

Tankleff's lawyer tried unsuccessfully to suppress the confession, but the youth was convicted of both murders and sentenced to two consecutive terms of twenty-five years to life. On direct appeal, the Appellate Division affirmed his conviction in a three-to-two decision. The Court of Appeals unanimously affirmed the decision upholding the conviction. The police are not required to be truthful.

Many other legal battles followed, some of them relating to the prosecution's peremptory challenges to strike all African American jurors. The defense also argued that the prosecution had failed to turn over potentially exculpatory evidence, such as information about the prior criminal activity of Steuerman, who they claimed had never been adequately investigated as a suspect. The case went all the way to the U.S. Supreme Court but lost there as well.

In 1989 the New York State Commission of Investigation (SIC) issued a public report, *An Investigation of the Suffolk County District*

Attorney's Office and Police Department, finding "grave shortcomings in the leadership and management of both agencies." The SIC said then district attorney Patrick Henry had "seriously failed in his stewardship as chief law enforcement officer in Suffolk County," and "the Suffolk County Police Department and District Attorney's Office engaged in and permitted improper practices to occur in homicide prosecutions, including perjury, as well as grossly deficient investigative and management practices." But this didn't change the result either.

A study by Richard Leo and Richard Ofshe cited *Tankleff* as a classic "false confession" case. (Further information about the case is available at http://www.angelfire.com/wy/tankleff/ or at http://www.freemarty.com.)

With Tankleff still in Clinton Correctional Facility, his counsel—Stephen L. Braga and Jennifer O'Connor of Baker Botts in Washington, D.C.—kept trying to point to discrepancies between the "confession" and the physical evidence. But some key witnesses were already dead, and most legal options had been exhausted. Hope from the courts was running out.

D.A. to review busts of bad cops
Schenectady

Drug cases handled by 2 disgraced officers under scrutiny; could affect scores of convictions

By Kim Martineau
Staff writer

The county's top prosecutor plans to order a sweeping review of some 2,000 felony drug cases his office has prosecuted over the last six years, based on admissions from two police officers that they doled out drugs to informers.

"This is something we have to do, no matter how time consuming or laborious, so this office will continue to have the confidence of the public," Schenectady County District Attorney Robert Carney said. "If we lose that, we lose everything."

The unprecedented review comes in the wake of guilty pleas by two former city patrol cops, Richard Barnett and Michael Siler, on corruption charges. The cases have raised a host of concerns that could undermine scores of convictions, including allegations of cops engaging in questionable arrest tactics. There are also concerns that a number of other officers may have engaged in similar practices, according to court documents.

Federal prosecutors believe that most of the cases Siler and Barnett worked on were legitimate. Carney said he thinks most of those cases will hold up under his review.

The FBI's probe into corruption on the police force has been ongoing for nearly two years, but it was only this week that details emerged as to how a group of rogue patrol cops, praised for the high number of arrests they made, routinely broke the law when dealing with informants. . . .

Convictions based on those types of arrests are vulnerable to being overturned because the officers could be accused of perjury, fabricating evidence or making a false arrest. . . .

—Reprinted with permission from the Albany *Times Union*, July 28, 2001, page A1

6

Police Misconduct

Sloppy, lazy, or fabricated police work is a common ingredient in wrongful convictions, but it seldom figures as a stated cause of reversals. That is because shoddy police investigation is neither a reversible error nor a harm that can be remedied by a tort or civil rights lawsuit. The law doesn't require the police to pursue every possible lead or piece of evidence, and once they have probable cause to arrest, they aren't legally required to continue their investigation, even if it is to clear the accused. Even where there is only arguable probable cause, police are generally protected from civil suits by virtue of qualified immunity.

Police misconduct periodically breaks into the headlines in the form of a sleazy police corruption scandal, sometimes involving frame-ups or evidence fabrication. Often the picture emerges of a tough cop who cuts corners and even violates the law in order to nab an unsavory suspect. But sometimes the reality is much worse. Honest cops rarely go against their dishonest fellow officers. Criminal defense attorneys constantly complain about officers who they believe lied on the stand or otherwise presented false evidence. Prosecutors, by contrast, prefer to raise their doubts in private if at all, and local, state, or federal prosecutions of police misconduct are extremely rare. Even when a conviction is tossed out by the courts in a way that further questions the veracity of the police officers and their supervisors, disciplinary action is not assured. There seldom is any follow-up to determine how crooked cops may have contributed to wrongful convictions.

New York

A Pattern of Brutality and Perjury

In 1998 inmate Jeffrey Santos was charged with second-degree assault against Corrections Captain Edward Lanza in the Manhattan House of Detention. Santos denied the charges, claiming that he had been repeatedly beaten by Lanza and as many as six other officers.

During the trial, defense counsel asked Lanza if he had been accused of using excessive force. The prosecutor objected, arguing that there was no basis to ask the question, and the judge instructed the jury to disregard the question. Santos was convicted and sentenced to six years of imprisonment.

After sentencing, however, appeals attorney Joanne Legano Ross of the Legal Aid Society learned that at the time of the incident, Captain Lanza was under active criminal investigation for assaulting numerous prisoners and falsifying records to conceal the assaults at Riker's Island's Punitive Segregation Unit. (He ultimately pleaded guilty in May 1999.) At the time of the Santos incident, Lanza was also the subject of a successful federal civil rights lawsuit regarding unnecessary use of force against prisoners. Yet neither the city, its Correction Department, nor the New York County DA had revealed any of this to the defense when Santos faced the assault charges. (The DA responded that he did not report it because he was unaware of the information, because the other assault case had occurred in Bronx County.)

In response to the 440.10 motion, on May 10, 2001, Acting Supreme Court Justice Dorothy A. Cropper vacated the judgment against Santos and ordered a new trial. "What is disturbing about the new evidence is that the prior instances of misconduct are so similar to the circumstances of the present case," she wrote.

Santos was released on bail, and the DA appealed Cropper's action. At this writing, Ross was preparing her respondent's brief for the Appellate Division.

Bronx

"Dropsey" Drug Evidence

In 1977, Laurence Solomon, a former professional baseball player with no prior criminal history, was arrested in Bronx County for criminal sale of a controlled substance, based on allegations by an undercover officer and an informer who had criminal charges pending against him. Solomon was convicted and sentenced to six years to life under the Rockefeller drug law.

Thirtieth Precinct Station House, Harlem. *New York Police Department.*

In 1979 his conviction was reversed as a result of prosecutorial misconduct. The Appellate Division cited numerous "inconsistencies" in the testimony of Special Agent Otto Privette of the New York Drug Enforcement Task Force, including discrepancies about whether the drugs were spotted after they had been dropped. On remand, Solomon was acquitted. In April 1992, the Court of Claims awarded him $187,050. Most allegations of "dropsey" evidence are never sustained.

New York

The Dirty Thirty

One of the biggest perjury scandals in the recent history of the New York Police Department came to light in the early 1990s, when it was shown that numerous police officers in a Harlem precinct had committed rampant crimes. A special city investigation by the Mollen Commission, followed up by the U.S. attorney for the Southern District and the Manhattan district attorney, revealed that between 1986 and 1994, no fewer than one-sixth of the cops in the Thirtieth Precinct routinely robbed drug dealers, fabricated evidence, committed perjury, and engaged in other crimes in the course of their official duties.

The systematic perjury was so pervasive that some cops sarcastically referred to it as "testilying." Yet, when the city's new police commissioner, William Bratton, inherited the scandal after a change in mayoral administration, he dismissed the prosecutors' public disclosures as self-serving "press-ti-lying," thereby suggesting that the prosecutors may have been trying to save face through the media.

The scandal forced prosecutors to throw out 125 convictions against ninety-eight individuals. But that number could have been much higher, as some insiders estimated that false police testimony had tainted the evidence in at least two thousand criminal cases. One cop alone admitted lying in seventy-five separate trials. As a result, the city paid millions of dollars in awards for false imprisonment. Thirty-three police officers were convicted and sentenced.

Many of the crooked cops got off easy. For example, a single perjury by Officer Stephen Pataki sent someone to prison for three years,
yet Officer Pataki drew only a three-month jail term. But officials had
revealed only the tip of the iceberg. Unlike the Knapp Commission of
the early 1970s, the probe was largely contained to the Thirtieth
Precinct. Insiders said that the powers-that-be had stopped the scandal
from implicating other precincts in order to spare the NYPD and the
legal system as a whole further embarrassment.

Joe Walsh, a former NYPD officer who served seven months in federal prison due to the probe, says as many as 60 percent of all arrests
may involve some form of police perjury. He says the most common
types involve drug or gun cases, particularly when police claim to have
seen something "in plain view."

Excerpts from the Mollen Report

"Police perjury and falsification of official records is a serious problem
facing the Department and the criminal justice system—largely because it
is often a 'tangled web' that officers weave to cover for other underlying
acts of corruption and wrongdoing."

"Officers also commit falsification to serve what they perceive as
'legitimate' law enforcement ends—and for ends that many honest and
corrupt officers alike stubbornly defend as correct. In their view, regardless of the legality of the arrest, the defendant is in fact guilty and ought
to be arrested. Officers reported a litany of manufactured tales. For
example, when officers unlawfully stop and search a vehicle because they
believe it contains drugs or guns, officers will falsely claim in police
reports and under oath that the car ran a red light (or committed some
other traffic violation) and that they subsequently saw contraband in the
car in plain view. To conceal an unlawful search of an individual who
officers believe is carrying drugs or a gun, they will falsely assert that
they saw a bulge in the person's pocket or saw drugs and money chang-
ing hands. To justify unlawfully entering an apartment where officers
believe narcotics or cash can be found, they pretend to have information

from an unidentified civilian informant or claim they saw the drugs in plain view after responding to the premises on a radio run. To arrest people they suspect are guilty of dealing drugs, they falsely assert that the defendants had drugs in their possession when, in fact, the drugs were found elsewhere where the officers had no lawful right to be."

"'Collars for Dollars' is a practice widely known to officers, police supervisors, and prosecutors alike. In fact, a confidential report prepared by a prosecutor's office involving a pattern of police falsification states that of the falsification arrests they investigated, '[a]lmost every arrest generated overtime pay for the officer who lied about observations.' Besides overtime pay, high arrest numbers are often a factor considered for coveted assignments for patrol officers and supervisors alike."

"Officers and their immediate supervisors are not the only culprits in tolerating falsifications. When officers believe that nothing is wrong with fabricating the basis of an arrest, a search, or other police action and that civil rights are merely an obstacle to aggressive law enforcement, the Department's top commanders must share the blame. . . . We are not aware of a single instance in which a supervisor or commander has been sanctioned for permitting perjury or falsification on their watch."

"[S]everal former and current prosecutors acknowledged—'off the record'—that perjury and falsifications are serious problems in law enforcement that, though not condoned, are ignored. The form this tolerance takes, however, is subtle which makes accountability in this area especially difficult. We have observed that provable cases of testimonial perjury are pursued in instances when the testimony of one eyewitness officer is squarely inconsistent with the testimony and reports of other officers and witnesses. In fact, in June 1993, the Manhattan District Attorney's Office obtained the conviction of a police officer who fabricated gun possession charges after the District Attorney's office noticed clear discrepancies in the officer's testimony."

"But the signs of falsification and perjury are usually far more subtle: a story that sounds suspicious to the trained ear; patterns of coincidences that are possible, but highly unlikely; inconsistencies that could be explained, but sound doubtful. In short, the tolerance the criminal justice system exhibits takes the form of a lesser level of scrutiny when it comes to police officers' testimony. Fewer questions are asked; weaker explanations are accepted."

—Commission to Investigate Allegations of Police Corruption and the Anti-Corruption Procedures of the Police Department, *Commission Report* (New York City, July 7, 1994)

CENTRAL INTELLIGENCE AGENCY
WASHINGTON, D.C. 20505

Office of General Counsel

1 March 1991

Barbara Campbell
Office of Liaison and International Affairs
Federal Bureau of Investigation
Washington, D.C. 20535

Dear Ms. Campbell:

In accordance with the past practice of our Office, I refer the enclosed information to you for lead purposes only. In addition, you may forward this information to appropriate local authorities if you deem such action appropriate. The individual admitted this information during security processing in connection with a prospective association with this Agency. As a consequence of this information, the individual was not accepted for the prospective position.

Should you need further information regarding this matter, please contact Mary Shiraishi of my Office at (703)   or secure .

Sincerely

Bernard Makowka
Deputy General Counsel
for Administrative Support

Enclosure

7

Fabrication of Evidence

There have been cases in which police have been found to have planted guns, supplied drugs, manufactured fingerprints, doctored reports, and engaged in other evidence fabrication practices. In most of them, even where the officers have admitted such actions, they have tried to claim that their targets were "really guilty" or "bad guys." Occasionally, episodes have been uncovered where the abuses were widespread and systematic. But even in those instances, no official attention has been paid to addressing the wrongful conviction implications of police corruption.

Broome, Chenango, Cortland, Delaware, Otsego, Tioga, Tompkins

The Great Fingerprint Scandal

In June 1992 a major police scandal started to break in central New York. The focus of the investigation involved fingerprint evidence—seemingly one of the irrefutable forms of criminal evidence—that apparently had been fabricated by the highly regarded New York State Police. The problem didn't come to light through administrative internal

Subject: David Lyle Harding
                SSN: 070-56-0598
                DPOB: 9 January 1958
                       Syre, Pa.

Last Known
Address: Box 131
                Cayuta Street
                Lockwood, N.Y. 14859

Business
Phone: (607) 563-9011
Home Phone: (607) 598-2621

    Harding is a New York State police officer. During
pre-employment processing, Harding volunteered the following
information regarding perjury in criminal prosecutions,
tampering with evidence in various criminal investigations, and
theft of State Government funds. According to Harding, other
officers were involved in these activities which occurred
between 1986 and 1990.

    Harding was involved in a homicide investigation in 1989.
He admitted to transplanting key evidence from one area to
another and that all subsequent reports, documents, and
testimony reflected that the evidence had been found in places
other than where it was actually found.

    According to Harding, he had testified in court on several
occasions that narcotics were discovered in locations covered
by search warrants when in fact the narcotics were found
elsewhere. In addition, he stated that he "planted" narcotics
on certain suspects. Harding also stated that he and other
officers had "padded the scales" when weighing narcotics to
increase the offence in several cases and in certain instances
lessened the weight of the narcotics found in order to give
some suspects a break. Although Harding denied taking
narcotics for personal use, he stated that another officer
would remove cocaine from evidence for personal use.

    Harding stated that he stole approximately $1,000 from
funds for a sting operation. His vouchers indicated he used
these funds to pay informants. He also extended motel rentals
used in sting operations to "entertain" women.

    Harding also admitted to having falsified court documents
during his divorce proceeding. He stated that he lied about
the amount of money he earned for the sale of certain property.

Internal CIA Communication. *Courtesy of New York State Special Prosecutor.*

CONSENT FOR POLYGRAPH EXAMINATION
(Applicant or Staff-Like Access)

I, ___David Lyle HARDING___ , consent to polygraph testing administered by examiners of the Central Intelligence Agency. I am under consideration for employment with the CIA or for staff-like access to Agency information or facilities. I understand that polygraph testing and periodic retesting is required as a condition of such employment or staff-like access.

The procedures that are to be followed during the examination have been explained to me, and I am aware that the procedures will include the use of sensors to record my physiological responses to questions. I understand that the questions to be asked during the examination will be only those questions necessary to resolve security suitability and counterintelligence issues, including but not limited to specific issues such as loyalty, the compromise of classified information, the falsification of personal history documents, vulnerability to blackmail or undue influence and involvement in criminal activity, and that the questions will be reviewed with me, at least in general, prior to the examination. I agree to keep the details of the examination secret from all unauthorized persons.

I am aware that information obtained in the course of the polygraph examination will be strictly controlled within the Central Intelligence Agency and may not be released outside of the Central Intelligence Agency except when necessary in the interest of national security as determined by the Director or Deputy Director of Central Intelligence, or as provided below.

I understand that any information relating to violations of law or an imminent threat to life or property may be reported to the Attorney General as required by Section 535 of Title 28 of the United States Code and Executive Order 12333 or its successors, and also may be reported to appropriate law enforcement or other government agencies for administrative, investigative, or legal action. I also understand I have a right against self-incrimination under the Fifth Amendment to the Constitution of the United States and that I may refuse to answer a question if my answer would tend to incriminate me. I understand that the session with the polygraph examiner may be monitored and is voice recorded for the purpose of clarity and accuracy. I understand that the session may be videotaped for the purpose of research and training.

I have read the foregoing and understand its import fully.

IN WITNESS WHEREOF, I place my signature below, this __14th__ day of ___January___ 19 __91__

SIGNATURE

The above was read and signed in my presence this __14th__ day of ___January___ 19 __91__

BY _____
S. GADA
TYPED TYPE

SIGNATURE

Internal CIA Communication. *Courtesy of New York State Special Prosecutor.*

controls, the crucible of the courtroom, or the vigilance of the news media. Only a fluke exposed it.

During a pre-employment interview with the Central Intelligence Agency in January 1991, Investigator David L. Harding of the state police had bragged that he had faked fingerprint evidence and committed perjury in court. His statements were verified by a hiring-related polygraph examination that was administered by the spy agency. Harding wasn't hired, but this information wasn't shared with the state police until sixteen months later.

Shortly after being notified of Harding's statements, on June 17, 1992 (the twentieth anniversary of the Watergate break-in), the state police sent inspectors to Langley, Virginia, to listen to the CIA's tape of Harding's interview. For the state police brass, one of the most worrisome aspects was Harding's claim that other division investigators had also fabricated criminal evidence to nab suspects.

Early in the investigation, and at the request of the state police, Tompkins County district attorney George Dentes was disqualified from prosecuting Harding due to a conflict of interest (they were friends), and Ithaca attorney Nelson E. Roth was handpicked as special prosecutor to look into the problem.

Special Prosecutor Reports Results

In January 1997, Roth reported the results of his investigation:

"For a period of at least eight years from 1984 to 1992, members of the New York State Police Troop C Identification Unit systematically violated their oaths of office, fabricated evidence, and committed perjury in approximately 40 criminal cases. Apparently coincidentally, a member of the State Police assigned to Troop F, in Middletown, New York, fabricated fingerprint evidence in at least two separate cases in 1991 and 1992.

"The misconduct occurred in cases originating in every county in Troop C, i.e., Broome, Chenango, Cortland, Delaware, Otsego, Tioga, and Tompkins Counties. The crimes involved ranged from the most serious, murder, rape, robbery, assault, and bombing, to burglaries, weapons charges, and drugs charges.

CONFIDENTIAL

REPORT TO THE HONORABLE GEORGE PATAKI

GOVERNOR OF THE STATE OF NEW YORK

PURSUANT TO SECTION SIX
OF THE NEW YORK STATE EXECUTIVE LAW

_____

THE NEW YORK STATE POLICE

EVIDENCE TAMPERING INVESTIGATION

NELSON E. ROTH

JANUARY 20, 1997
ITHACA, NEW YORK

Special prosecutor's report. *New York State Special Prosecutor.*

"Tainted evidence was found in at least 34 cases in Troop C and in seven or eight additional cases fabrication is either likely or cannot be eliminated as a possibility. Fingerprint 'fabrications' were accomplished in a variety of ways, some quite sophisticated. The methodologies included (1) simply lying about the source of a legitimate print, claiming it came from one location generally incriminating to the suspect rather than its actual source; (2) using the same method as (1), but having the defendant touch an object while in police custody so that his prints could be obtained to frame him; (3) lifting an ink impression from an inked fingerprint card, perhaps doctoring its appearance, and claiming that it was a latent lift taken from a crime scene; (4) making copies of ink impressions, using a variety of methods, and making lifts from the copies; (5) manipulating photographic negatives to produce photographs of latents and/or ink impressions and also depicting a background different than the actual source of the 'print'; and (6) making 'lifts' directly from the fingers of a dead homicide victim and doctoring their appearance so as to be able to use them at a later time to 'plant' as evidence against a suspect, i.e., to place the victim, through his fingerprints, in proximity to the suspect (such as in his car or residence).

"Notwithstanding the fact that the corruption continued for at least eight years, involved dozens of cases, and spanned three generations of ID personnel, and notwithstanding the fact that one of the first participants, if not the first, later supervised the ID Unit as the BCI Lieutenant during a time when the corruption continued and grew unabated, all participants have essentially denied that there was any type of organized plan, that they communicated with one another about the fabrications and perjury (except in a few instances), that they were taught by anybody else, that they taught anybody else, or that they were aware of the misconduct of others. These claims are very difficult to believe. They also make it difficult to confirm the identities of the originator(s) of the misconduct or how the misconduct was perpetuated.

"Questions have been raised by members of the public, the defense bar, and the media about the possible role of district attorneys in the entire affair. . . . [M]any questions have been raised about the conduct of Tompkins County District Attorney George Dentes. . . . These questions have also been generated in part by the appearance of a close relationship between Mr. Dentes and David Harding [the central figure in the scandal]. . . . [A]t the very least, the prosecutor's use of Harding's perjurious testimony concerning fabricated evidence is without justification. It reflects an insensitivity by the prosecutor to the duty to ensure that any criminal proceeding is untainted by perjurious testimony and fabricated evidence."
—Nelson E. Roth, confidential report to the Honorable George Pataki, Governor of the State of New York, *Pursuant to Section Six of the New*

York State Executive Law: the New York State Evidence Tampering Investigation (Ithaca, New York, January 20, 1997)

Behind the Scenes

In an interview for this book, Roth praised state police high commanders for responding to the abuses "with a vengeance." But he recalled that his internal briefing to the troop commanders was greeted by "stony silence."

In the end, his report also found that a labor union representing investigators (the New York State Police Investigators Association) "played an intentionally hostile and destructive role" and took steps to "undermine the investigation." Roth says he was "dismayed" by a number of the rank and file who "didn't seem to be disturbed [as he was] by the taint" the episode had placed on the state police.

Nobody knows how many convictions were ultimately lost as an outgrowth of the great fingerprint scandal. Nobody kept track. According to Roth, most of the fabricated evidence was used against persons who were "actually guilty," but he concedes that at least some of those affected were wrongly accused. He admits that wrongful conviction of innocent persons was "obviously not the focus of the investigation. Pretty much the farthest we went was to notify district attorneys and defense counsel, and then we moved on. And I don't recall that there was any response from the DAs Association." Some defendants later complained that their defense counsel had not adequately responded either, and at least on of them sued her former lawyer for not filing civil lawsuits on her behalf.

Roth says the most chilling case he encountered involved the unsolved murder of young Jimmy Bernardo, a twelve-year-old Pittsfield boy whose corpse had been found in the town of Newfield. In the state police file, investigators found a set of fingerprint impressions that had been taken from the boy's remains and specially prepared for possible use in a future fabrication. As it turned out, fingerprints were not used to convict the boy's killer, Lewis Lent, when he was prosecuted several years later. But Roth adds, "They could have been used to implicate someone, including the wrong man."

Queens

A Reporter Uncovers Frame-Ups

Bertram Campbell, a respected Wall Street customer's man, was convicted of forgery and served four years in Sing Sing before his conviction was thrown out after it was discovered what methods the police had used to identify him as the perpetrator. In 1945 it was revealed that that police had showed three of the five identifying witnesses a "doctored" photograph of Campbell, in which a moustache had been dubbed in to match the criminal's description. He had also been paraded in front of witnesses before the lineup and identified as a front man for a forgery ring.

In 1948 the case helped prompt a study by the New York State Judicial Council, which reported:

> Were the Campbell case merely an isolated instance, it would still furnish cause for inquiry into the possibility of improving methods of identification. Our civilization is grounded upon the sanctity of individual rights. More than lip service should be paid to the adage that it is better that a guilty person go free than an innocent person should be punished. Unfortunately, however, there have been more Campbell cases than is generally realized. The annals of criminal law contain a number of miscarriages of justice resulting from erroneous identification.

Ed Mowery reported about the Campbell case in the New York *World-Telegram*. Mowery's stories helped Campbell win a pardon from Governor Thomas Dewey and $115,000 in damages from New York State in 1946. As a result, Mowery was deluged with letters from prisoners, alleging other cases of wrongful conviction. One of them involved a penniless Brooklyn clerk, Louis Hoffner, who was serving a life term for murdering a Queens bartender during a robbery.

From 1947 to 1952, Mowery produced seventy stories for the *World-Telegram and Sun*, showing Hoffner's innocence. The reporter got seven of the trial jurors to request a new trial. He also documented the judge's confusing charge to the jury, unearthed evidence of police perjury and coercion, obtained affidavits from missing alibi witnesses, and found another eyewitness to the murder. Mowery dug up secret police records revealing that the main witness against Hoffner had failed to identify him in a lineup, until the police had coached him to do so in a second lineup.

In 1952, Hoffner's conviction was overturned, and a judge granted the prosecutor's motion to dismiss the indictment. Hoffner was freed from prison. For his efforts, Mowery received the Pulitzer Prize for Local Reporting in 1953.

Suffolk

Finding the "Magic Bullet"

Charles Hamilton, age nineteen, was convicted of second-degree murder and first-degree robbery in Suffolk County in 1982 and sentenced to twenty-five years to life.

The arresting officer, Detective Dennis Rafferty of the Suffolk Police Department, claimed to have obtained a full, signed confession. Hamilton maintained the confession was false and swore he had never signed it. Seven months after the arrest, Officer Rafferty also suddenly claimed to have found a critical piece of physical evidence in Hamilton's pocket at the time of his arrest. It was a twenty-two caliber Winchester Western bullet that Suffolk police said matched a shell in the murder. The prosecution's ballistics expert testified that he found markings on this bullet that matched markings on the expended casing found at the crime scene, indicating that, at some point, each bullet had been chambered in the same weapon.

Charles Hamilton. *Courtesy of Charles Hamilton.*

Hamilton claimed the bullet had been planted, saying the bullet in question had not been reported by Rafferty at the time of the arrest. Hamilton's lawyer later discovered that a bullet of the same description had been vouchered as having been received a month before Hamilton's arrest, and the police could no longer account for its whereabouts.

Hamilton's confession was ruled inadmissible, however the bullet proved the only physical evidence linking Hamilton to the crime and was crucial in the jury's finding of guilt.

Years later, Detective Rafferty's conduct in homicide cases was specifically cited by the State Commission of Investigation in a public report, *An Investigation of the Suffolk County District Attorney's Office and Police Department* (1989), that questioned Rafferty's role in obtaining other purported confessions and his handling of other key evidence. (His police work has since been questioned in other cases as well.) The SIC report documented many other abuses by Suffolk County police and prosecutors, including the manufacturing of evidence, knowingly allowing false testimony, tailoring testimony to fit fabricated evidence, withholding evidence favorable to the defense, and collusion by police and prosecutors in covering up these practices.

After Hamilton's conviction was affirmed, Rafferty was disciplined for mishandling the bullet in question, and he was transferred from the Homicide Division to the Robbery Division.

Charles Hamilton today. *Courtesy of the Hamilton family.*

Paul Gianelli of Hauppauge, the private attorney who had represented Hamilton at trial, later wrote to him in 1997, saying, "Although almost 15 years has gone by since I have represented you, I believe just as firmly today as I did then that you would not have been convicted had it not been for this testimony by Detective Rafferty that he found the .22 caliber bullet in your pocket on the day that he arrested you."

In 2000, Hamilton filed a 440.10 motion to vacate his conviction, but the motion was denied. In 2001 his lawyer filed an application for leave to appeal the denial of his motion, but this application was denied. This meant all of Hamilton's state remedies were exhausted.

Hamilton remained in prison. His appeals lawyer, Charlita Mays, kept fighting the case in federal court, seeking federal review of his habeas corpus claim on the grounds of "actual innocence." Although, under the Anti-Terrorism Act and Effective Death Penalty Act of 1996, persons whose convictions became final before April 24, 1996, had one year to file a petition for a writ of habeas corpus, and Hamilton was clearly outside that time frame, his counsel argued that if a claim of actual innocence is properly raised and established, the court is obliged to decide it. Counsel argued that the prosecution's withholding of material and the discovery of new evidence demonstrated that he was deprived of a fair trial in violation of his constitutional rights under the Fourteenth Amendment. At this writing, Charles Hamilton is still behind bars for a crime he did not commit.

**STATE OF NEW YORK
COMMISSION OF INVESTIGATION**

AN INVESTIGATION OF THE SUFFOLK COUNTY

DISTRICT ATTORNEY'S OFFICE

AND POLICE DEPARTMENT

April 1989

270 BROADWAY
NEW YORK, NEW YORK 10007

Suffolk County investigation report.
New York State Commission of Investigation.

Key frame from a suppressed and doctored prosecution video in the Bermudez case. *Courtesy of Fernando Bermudez.*

8

Prosecutorial Misconduct

Prosecutors enjoy the power to make potential life or death decisions, and to ruin or preserve careers. Most of this decision making takes place behind closed doors and without outside scrutiny. The main way they are held accountable is through the electoral process, and most DAs are easily reelected.

The U.S. Supreme Court has ruled that a prosecutor is entitled to absolute immunity from "harassing litigation that would divert his time and attention from his official duties." Some question the wisdom of granting absolute immunity to prosecutors when they have violated constitutional rights. Professor Adele Bernhard contends, "If prosecutors have acted negligently and haven't taken the time to investigate information, there's no reason not to hold them responsible. Everybody else in society has to bear responsibility for his or her decision-making. Why should prosecutors be so very different?" Another Pace professor who specializes in prosecution issues, Professor Bennett Gershman, calls prosecutorial misconduct "a serious cancer in our system of justice," adding, "There is no check on prosecutorial misconduct except for the prosecutor's own attitudes and beliefs and inner morality."

In New York, efforts to pass legislation holding prosecutors more accountable have failed. Their chief sponsor, Assemblyman Sam Colman of the Ninety-third District, insists, "In most cases where an innocent person has ended up in jail, the prosecutor has been overzealous. Don't forget—their job is to seek justice, not convictions. But DAs are very arrogant people. I'd like to see them held more accountable." Colman wants to make prosecutors subject to a strict code of conduct enforced by an independent board, modeled after the system that governs judges. But most lawmakers are afraid to cross the powerful prosecutors. The DAs Association rules the roost.

Kings

The Fire Next Time

On the morning of August 2, 1978, six city firemen were killed fighting a blaze at Waldbaum's Supermarket in Brooklyn. In the wake of the tragedy, Erick Jackson was arrested. The evidence linking him to the fire was his alleged "confession" to Julio Cruz, Detective Harold J. Harmon, and former assistant district attorney Michael Gary. The "confession"

Doomed firefighters on Waldbaum's roof. *Courtesy of Robert Sullivan.*

stated that the defendant and two others had climbed up to the roof, where the defendant and his companions made holes and threw in paper doused with lighter fluid, setting it ablaze. The confession said that after the fire was going well, he and his companions fled. Authorities said Jackson stated that he had received $1,500 or $500 to set fire to Waldbaum's.

During the trial, Fire Marshal Charles King testified he had found four separate points of origin of the fires, clearly indicating arson as the cause.

On December 1, 1980, a jury convicted Jackson of second-degree arson and six counts of felony murder stemming from the fire. On March 2, 1981, he was sentenced to twenty-five years to life. The conviction was affirmed by the Court of Appeals.

After information was discovered that had not been disclosed to the defense, the trial court ruled that a per se violation of law required *vacatur* of the conviction without a showing of prejudice, and the Appellate Division affirmed its decision.

But in 1991 the Court of Appeals, in a four-to-three decision, reversed. Its surprise ruling represented a stunning setback for defense lawyers. At the heart of the decision was the requirement that any prior statement of a prosecution witness must be turned over to the defense before trial. Until the new decision, any failure to do so was grounds for an automatic reversal. The opinion, written by Chief Judge Sol Wachtler, diluted this safeguard by holding that reversal was required only when a case had actually been prejudiced by the violation. Civil libertarians were aghast.

The criminal case seemed over until the firefighters' widows hired an attorney, Robert G. Sullivan of Sullivan and Lipakis, P.C., to bring a suit for civil damages. Sullivan quickly established that the original fire probably had not been caused by arson but by faulty electrical wiring. Following up on the four separate points of origin, he determined that the "arson" had been committed later—by members of the fire department, in order to aid the families of the deceased firefighting personnel by helping their benefits case. Sullivan also showed that members of the police department and the fire department had known of this and reported it to the prosecutor, but the prosecutor had covered it up and prosecuted Jackson instead. The district attorney's office had also withheld other crucial, extensive exculpatory information, some of it bearing on Jackson's "confession." Based on what he found, Sullivan tried to gain Jackson's release.

After reviewing the evidence, the original trial judge, Supreme Court Justice Joseph Slavin, threw out the conviction, saying: "The Court finds that society was the loser in this trial. The Jury had but a small part of the information necessary for determination of the defendant's guilt or innocence. A fair trial was not had on this matter." He added, "The greatest crime of all in a civilized society is an unjust conviction. It is truly a scandal, which reflects unfavorably on all the participants in the criminal justice system. . . . No one is entitled to a perfect trial but everyone is entitled to a fair trial. . . . Jackson did not receive that fair trial. The pity is that it took . . . eleven years to reach this result."

Erick Jackson's conviction was vacated, and he was released from prison on November 3, 1988, after serving ten years. But the Jackson story didn't end there.

Aftermath

Jackson made the mistake of remaining in Brooklyn. A few years later, the police pursued him again. This time it was for a series of rapes, but the DNA didn't match. Then police produced a witness—a prostitute. The prosecution said Jackson had approached her seeking used condoms, containing human sperm and DNA from other men, that he could leave behind at his serial rapes, in order to divert attention from himself. But when the witness took the stand, she shocked the court by denying the allegations, saying the police had tried to get her to commit perjury. As a result, Jackson was acquitted. Police and prosecutors were furious.

No legal action was taken against any of the responsible officials in either case.

In fact, the city fire commissioner from 1980 to 1983, Charles J. (Joe) Hynes, later became special prosecutor for law enforcement and failed to pursue the allegations about the fire department's wrongdoing. After becoming district attorney of King's County in 1989, Hynes pro-

Robert Sullivan. *Courtesy of Robert Sullivan.*

ceeded with the retrial against Jackson, despite evidence that Jackson
was innocent, and his office later prosecuted Jackson again for rape.
Hynes ran for governor in 1998 and lost. He has continued to be reelected as DA, most recently in 2001.

Another prosecutor in the case, Jon Besunder, became deputy chief
of the homicide bureau under District Attorney Hynes.

Charles Gary, the assistant district attorney who prosecuted
Jackson for the fire, later became a supreme court judge in Kings
County.

The bureau chief who received a memorandum about the electrical
nature of the fire and helped conceal it from the defense was Richard
Aiello, who went on to become administrative judge for Brooklyn and
Staten Island.

New York

The Story of Isidore Zimmerman

One of the most famous wrongful conviction cases in New York history involved Isidore (Beansy) Zimmerman, who was arrested with four others for the murder of police detective Michael Foley in New York in 1937. Although no evidence indicated Zimmerman's direct involvement, he was accused of serving as an "accessory before the fact," which made him liable for a charge of capital murder. After a twenty-day trial before Judge Charles Nott (known as one of the toughest judges in the state), Zimmerman was convicted and sentenced to death. The Court of Appeals affirmed his conviction, although noting that he had not been at the scene of the crime.

Three of the convicted killers were put to death. But within an hour of Zimmerman's scheduled execution, Governor Herbert Lehman commuted his sentence to life.

Years later, lawyer Maurice Edelbaum took up Zimmerman's case on a *pro bono* basis. Finally, in 1962, the Court of Appeals granted a writ of *coram nobis*, reversing his conviction and ordering a new trial, finding that the prosecutor, Jacob J. Rosenblum, had willfully suppressed evidence that Zimmerman was innocent. Shortly afterward, the charges were dismissed and Zimmerman was released.

Zimmerman, who had served twenty-four years for a crime he didn't commit, spent several more years fighting to clear his name. He wrote a book about his experience, *Punishment without Crime*, and tried to recover damages. After years of lobbying, he finally convinced Governor Hugh Carey to sign legislation granting him permission to sue the state. In 1982 the Court of Claims awarded Zimmerman $1 million. But he died of a heart attack a few months later. In 1984, under Governor Mario M. Cuomo, New York State enacted the Wrongful Conviction and Imprisonment Act, which is often called the Zimmerman law after Isidore Zimmerman.

Charles Sberna. *Author's photo.*

NAME:	Charles Sberna, 95–270
AGE:	29
OCCUPATION:	Upholsterer
EDUCATION:	7th grade
CRIME:	Shot Patrolman John Wilson, street, holdup, 9–23–37
ACCOMPLICE:	Salvatore Gati 95–271
CLAIMS:	Denies guilt
JUDGE:	John Wallace, NY General Sessions
SENTENCED:	7–7–38
EXECUTED:	1–5–39

New York

All the Way to the Chair

Two parolees, Charles Sberna and Salvatore Gati, were charged with murdering Officer John A. Wilson in Manhattan during a gold refinery robbery on September 23, 1937. An unidentified accomplice had escaped.

Gati later testified that Sberna was innocent, and Sberna denied his guilt, but both men were convicted and sentenced to death.

A presentence investigation report for Sberna dated September 20, 1938, noted, "His wife says that she knows positively that her husband is innocent. She says Gati, #95271 confided this information to his sisters and that they in turn told her but they refuse to put it on the record because the 2 other men implicated in the murder have large families while inmate Sberna has none . . . the other [implicated man] is John Lepore who was formerly in Sing Sing but has since transferred to Auburn Prison."

At the death house, another wrongfully condemned prisoner, Isidore Zimmerman, also became convinced that Sberna was innocent. Zimmerman claimed that the chief of the Homicide Bureau for the New York district attorney, Jacob J. Rosenblum, had been instrumental in falsely convicting both himself and Sberna, despite knowing they were innocent.

On September 26, 1938, Sing Sing's Catholic chaplain, John P. McCaffrey, appealed to Warden Lewis E. Lawes, saying, "This is the first time I've ever been positive that an innocent man was going to the chair, and there is nothing I can do about it. If only people would make sure they know what they are talking about before they swear a man's life away."

Sberna and Gati were legally executed at Sing Sing on January 5, 1939. Sberna was not the first or the last wrongfully convicted person to be executed in New York.

Bronx

"It Would Seem . . . Tacitly Obvious"

Larry Boone was convicted of murder in Bronx County in 1973 and sentenced to twenty-five years to life. In 1975 the conviction was reversed because the prosecutor had failed to disclose crucial exculpatory evidence, and all charges were dropped. The Court of Claims granted Boone's summary judgment on his wrongful imprisonment claim. But before the case was settled, Boone died.

The Court of Claims judge who handled the case concluded that Boone had "shown by clear and convincing evidence that he was innocent of the crime for which he was imprisoned." On that judge's retirement, however, the question of damages was taken up by a replacement.

In March 1992, Court of Claims Judge Donald J. Corbett Jr. expressed no sympathy for what Boone may have suffered as a result of his wrongful conviction. Corbett concluded:

> It would seem, at first glance, tacitly obvious that one convicted of murder would suffer a loss of reputation. Unfortunately, without Claimant's direct testimony (and his deposition testimony is unavailing), the record is devoid of any evidence that Claimant was looked upon less favorably by friends and acquaintances as a result of his conviction.

Corbett awarded only $45,000 to the administrator of Boone's estate.

Albany

A Claimant's Damage Assessment

William Chapman was convicted of arson and attempted murder in Albany County and sentenced to twenty-five years to life. He served three years and nine months in prison before the Appellate Division, Third Department, reversed the conviction on the grounds of insufficient evidence and dismissed the indictment, finding that he was not culpable.

Chapman then filed a claim under Section 8-b of the Court of Claims Act, seeking the following:

(a) For imprisonment, loss of freedom, detention and confinement from May 15, 1984 to February 19, 1988—$3,500,000.
(b) For injury to reputation, shame and humiliation, indignity and disgrace, ridicule and scorn—$750,000.
(c) For mental anguish and suffering—$750,000.

(d) For loss of enjoyment of life, including loss of the company of family, friends, and disturbance of everyday living— $350,000.

(e) For pecuniary losses, including loss of earnings and opportunities for employment and impairment of employability— $65,000.

(f) For expenses of defending charges and securing release, including investigating legal services—$6,500.

(g) Total damages—$5,421,500.

In December 1993, the Court of Claims awarded Chapman $50,000.

New York

The Tale of the Tape

Fernando Bermudez was accused of murdering another youth after a party at a Union Square dancehall in 1991. Five strangers identified him as the shooter. Represented at trial by private counsel, he was prosecuted by New York ADA James G. Rodriguez. Although there was no physical evidence against him, and despite presenting alibi witnesses, Bermudez was convicted of second-degree murder. Supreme Court Justice John A. K. Bradley sentenced him to twenty-three years to life.

After his conviction, Bermudez's father, Frank, a Dominican immigrant, helped mount an investigation. His new lawyer, Mary Ann DiBari, personally went into the streets seeking critical information. Her investigation proved fruitful. DiBari obtained affidavits from five prosecution witnesses recanting their identifications of Bermudez and suggesting that police identification procedures had been unduly suggestive and involved improper threats and pressure. She also argued that the prosecutor had failed to fulfill his disclosure obligations and pressured witnesses to testify against Bermudez. And she claimed that newly discovered evidence supported his innocence.

DiBari discovered that a videotape of the police identification procedures had been doctored before it was turned over to the defense.

After obtaining an unedited version, she argued that the deleted section had contained both exculpatory information and information that could have helped investigators find the real killer.

Fernando Bermudez and his family. *Courtesy of Fernando Bermudez.*

The prosecution refused to yield, however, and Justice Bradley confiscated the tape and denied the motion, siding with the authorities. The Appellate Division, First Department, upheld the conviction and the Court of Appeals denied both leave to appeal and a motion for reconsideration.

Bermudez filed two additional postconviction proceedings, which were also denied by the Appellate Division and Judge Bradley. His lawyer's efforts received strong coverage from *Newsday*, a local television station, and NBC National News, but to no avail.

His new lawyer, Marjorie Smith, filed a petition for a writ of habeas corpus before U.S. magistrate Judge Kevin Fox in the Southern District of New York. In it, Bermudez claimed his constitutional rights were violated by the state's use of impermissibly suggestive identification procedures, its failure to disclose exculpatory evidence and documents, prosecutorial misconduct, the use of perjured evidence at trial, and the ineffectiveness of trial and appellate counsel. At the heart of the case, counsel claimed the witnesses misidentified him from a police mug shot, due to suggestive police procedures and because he strongly resembled a gang leader. Bermudez claimed the videotape actually includes the name of the person they named as the killer. But at this writing, Bermudez remained in prison, awaiting action by the federal court, which had already taken nearly five months to consider his arguments.

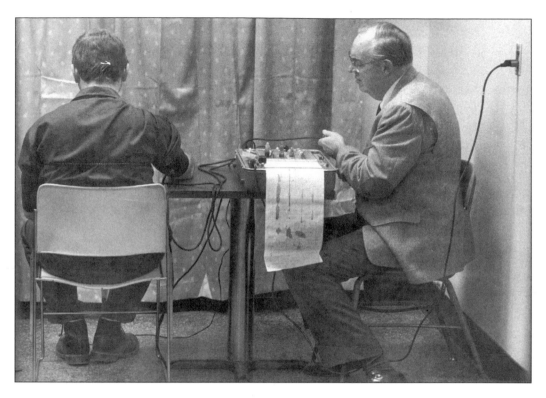

Polygraph expert Warren Holmes of Maine tests an inmate at
New York's Auburn Prison. *Courtesy of the Rochester Democrat and Chronicle.*

9

Forensics

For more than a century, progressively newer forensic investigation techniques have given law enforcement more powerful scientific tools to solve crimes. Proponents of fingerprinting, ballistics, microscopic hair and fiber comparison, polygraphy, forensic dentistry, serology inclusion, and, most recently, DNA all have offered almost magical new methods to obtain graphic and strong physical evidence of guilt—or innocence. Depending on the extent to which the courts have allowed their use as legal evidence, some of these techniques have had a significant impact on who is arrested, convicted, or cleared. Yet each technique has its own limitations and potential for abuse.

Forensic evidence can be used to help obtain a conviction or to help overturn one. DNA has proven to be especially potent in this regard. Although polygraph test results have remained inadmissible at trial since *Frye v. United States* (1923), defense attorneys have succeeded at using such evidence to help convince some prosecutors to dismiss an indictment—in conjunction with other compelling evidence supporting innocence.

Fingerprint Evidence under Scrutiny

Since 1911, New York courts have generally accepted fingerprint evidence as admissible scientific evidence, provided it is done according to established procedures. New York State has long been a world leader in the use of fingerprint data banks to help identify criminals. A few years ago, the state converted to a multimillion-dollar, state-of-the-art computerized fingerprint system that harnesses new technology as a crime-fighting tool to match prints against millions of active criminal history files.

New York Police Department.

But recent legal challenges have questioned the infallibility of what seemed to be the established use of fingerprinting. Defense lawyers contend that fingerprint identification techniques have not been held up to scientific scrutiny. In 1993, in *Daubert v. Merrell Dow Pharmaceuticals*, the U.S. Supreme Court required federal judges to determine the reliability of expert testimony, and this has prompted some defense attorneys to push for evidentiary hearings to challenge fingerprint evidence.

Several leading scholars—including Simon F. Cole, author of *Suspect Identities: A History of Fingerprinting and Criminal Identification* (2001)—now contend that the standard error rates surrounding fingerprint analysis may cause prosecutors to place greater reliance on DNA. Recent challenges have also focused on the proficiency of individual fingerprint takers and examiners, claiming that they are not sufficiently skilled or scientific. As a result, they say, fingerprint identification is a "subjective determination."

Noting such instances as the great fingerprint scandal in New York referred to earlier in this book, Cole also points to fingerprinting's susceptibility for fabrication as a serious problem. "The history of fabrications shows that it's always been the cops who've been doing it—and never the alleged criminals who are trying to divert suspicion," he says in an interview. "Fabrications may have been rather easy to get away with because nobody, from the police, to the prosecution, DCJS [the state Division of Criminal Justice Services], or the defense, really reviewed such evidence. In fact, the adversarial system has not been vigilant."

Orleans

Bad and Good Ballistics

The new forensic science of ballistics was in its infancy in 1915 when a prosecutor used it with a confession and other seemingly airtight evidence to convict Charles Stielow and Nelson Green of a double murder in Shelby, Orleans County. Green's guilty plea had earned him a life sentence, but Stielow, a German immigrant, was convicted at trial and sentenced to death in the electric chair.

Shortly afterward, however, Sing Sing prison officials became convinced that Stielow was innocent, and they alerted some reformers. Their initial investigation made the case a cause célèbre that rallied journalists, feminists, private detectives, scientists, and even sleuths from Scotland Yard. At least two early filmmakers, including D. W. Griffith, used the case as the basis for a moving picture.

The governor at the time, Charles Whitman, was a former Manhattan district attorney who was still under criticism for two recent disputed capital convictions (Thomas Bambrick and Charles Becker). In response to the pressure, Whitman granted a last-minute stay of execution and later commuted the sentence to life. But it would take his appointment of a state special prosecutor and a state-of-the-art reinvestigation to undo the wrongful convictions.

The special prosecutor used a team of ballistics experts to prove that the previous bullet testimony was fraudulent, and newly devised scientific tests showed that the gun in question had not fired the fatal shots. The investigators also exposed Stielow's confession as false and the product of extreme coercion, and they even obtained valid confessions from the real killers, who happened to be associates of the Orleans district attorney.

Stielow and Green were exonerated, but the real murderers were never brought to justice because local residents refused to indict them, out of embarrassment, resentment about outside interference, and an unwillingness to have to pay for another expensive trial.

Bronx

DNA to the Rescue

Marion Coakley was convicted of rape and robbery in Bronx County in 1983, after the victim picked out Coakley's photograph at the police precinct and later fingered him in a police lineup. Three eyewitnesses incorrectly identified Coakley as the perpetrator. Despite producing eight alibi witnesses and passing a lie detector test, Coakley was found guilty by a jury and sentenced to five to fifteen years.

From *left*, Barry Scheck, Peter Neufeld, and Jim Dwyer. *Courtesy of Peter Neufeld.*

His appeals attorney belatedly discovered that the prosecution had concealed knowledge that the victim and her primary eyewitness had filed a $10 million civil suit against the motel where the crime allegedly had occurred, as well as that the motel management had alleged the pair had concocted the story of the rape as a pretext for suing the motel for negligence. Also, the victim's psychiatric history raised doubts about her credibility. A chambermaid at the motel had seen another person fitting the description of the perpetrator and failed to identify Coakley as that person, yet this also had been withheld from the defense. The police had failed to pursue other suspects.

After his postconviction counsel turned up this newly discovered evidence, and additional DNA tests positively ruled out Coakley as the perpetrator, the court set aside his conviction and the Bronx district attorney dismissed the indictment in the interests of justice. Coakley was released in 1987.

On March 31, 1994 the Court of Claims awarded him $450,000.

Coakley's case was included in the best-selling book *Actual Innocence: When Justice Goes Wrong and How to Make It Right (2000)*, by Barry Scheck, Peter Neufeld, and Jim Dwyer, as well as in a law review article about indemnification for unjust conviction, written by Adele Bernhard of Pace University School of Law.

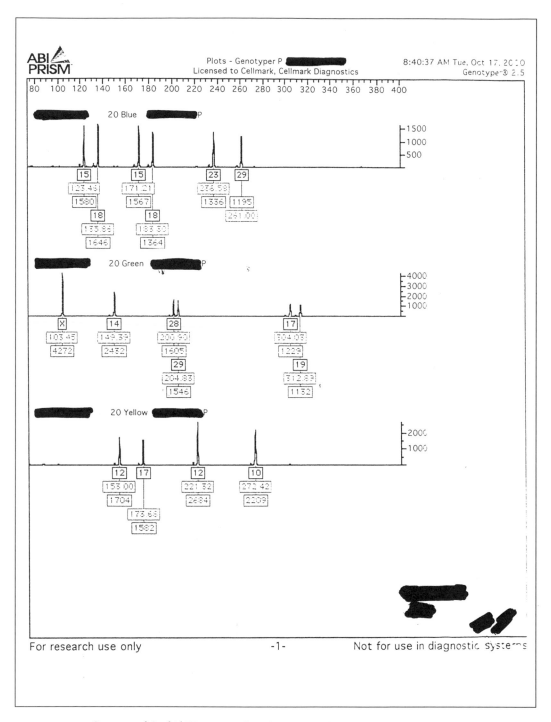

Courtesy of Orchid Biosciences, Inc., Princeton N.J.

160

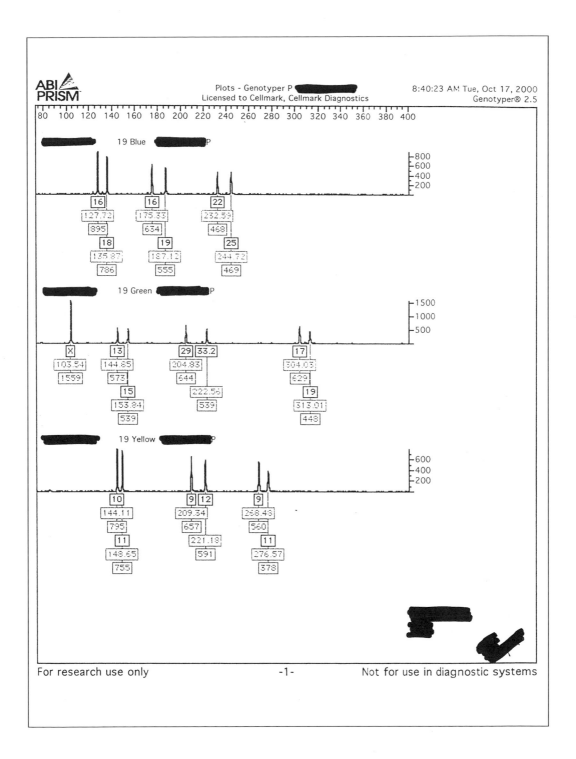

Westchester

Polymerase Chain Reaction

Terry Leon Chalmers was arrested for rape in Westchester County in 1986 after two victims picked out his picture from a photo array. He was also identified in two lineups. He was convicted of rape in Westchester County in 1987 and sentenced to twelve to twenty-four years. His conviction was upheld by the Appellate Division, Second Department, in 1990.

With assistance by the Innocence Project at Yeshiva University's Cardozo Law School, however, the conviction was reversed and the indictment dismissed in 1995 after newly discovered DNA proved he was innocent. As recounted in Chalmers's verified claim for damages:

> On April 20, 1994, Judge West granted claimant's request to release four rape kit swabs from the victim of the August 18, 1986 sexual assault for purposes of DNA testing. . . . These swabs were sent to Dr. Edward T. Blake of Forensic Science Associates (FSA) of Richmond, California. Dr. Blake was the first criminalist to apply the technique of polymerase chain reaction (PCR) to test forensic samples. He has achieved national recognition from his peers in the scientific community, and courts throughout the world, as a pioneer and leading practitioner of forensic DNA testing.
>
> Dr. Blake tested two of the swabs—a cervical and vaginal swab—determined they contained sperm, and typed them using the DQ Alpha and Polymarker DNA testing systems. He reported the results of those tests in a July 8, 1994 report before he tested the reference sample of claimant. In this respect, Dr. Blake's initial testing of the forensic samples was done "blind"; i.e., without knowledge of claimant's DNA profile for the systems being employed. . . .
>
> After receiving claimant's reference sample and typing it, Dr. Blake reported on July 26, 1994 that claimant's DNA profile did not match the DNA profile of the sperm donor on the cervical and vaginal swabs on three different genetic marker systems (the GYPA, HBGG, and GC markers).

The prosecution sent the remaining swabs to a laboratory of their own choosing, Geneflex, which replicated Blake's results. The prosecution also notified the victim of the August 18 rape and confirmed from her that the sperm on the swabs could not have come from anyone but the rapist.

Orange

Conditions of Confinement

Victor Ortiz was convicted of felonious rape and sodomy in Orange County in 1984 and sentenced to twelve and a half to twenty-five years. After he had served approximately thirteen years in ten maximum-security facilities, newly discovered DNA evidence proved he was innocent, resulting in the overturn of his conviction; he was released.

In June 1997 he received a total of $560,905.96 from the Court of Claims, which ruled:

> Claimant described the sparse furnishings and sanitary conditions of a typical cell, the shower facilities, lockdown and search procedures, the meals and a typical day as an inmate. He testified that is especially difficult and lonely for an inmate imprisoned for a sexual offense. Claimant testified that his cell was set on fire twice while he was imprisoned, and he was severely beaten on one occasion in January 1989, which required his hospitalization. Claimant was hospitalized for one night in connection with the attack and remained in the infirmary at Sing Sing for about six weeks thereafter. After his discharge from the infirmary, claimant was housed in protective custody. He described the condition of a cell in protective custody, and explained that inmates spend 23 hours per day in the cell with one hour of outside recreation. He remained in protective custody for seven years. Claimant testified that because of his incarceration, he was unable to attend his father's funeral in January 1990.
>
> —From the decision by Judge Andrew P. O'Rourke,
> Court of Claims, Claim No. 96390, March 28, 2000

Suffolk

Kerry Kotler

Kerry Kotler was convicted of rape in Suffolk County in 1981 and sentenced to twenty-five to fifty years. The conviction was reversed and the charges dismissed in 1992, based on newly discovered DNA evidence, after Kotler had served eleven years in prison. The chief prosecution expert who conducted the serology tests that convicted him pleaded guilty to perjury charges for lying about his qualifications and training. On June 30, 1997, Kotler received $1,510,000 from the Court of Claims. Four months later, Kotler was sentenced to eight and a third to twenty-five years for another rape committed three years after his release from prison.

Erie

Winning by a Hair

Attorney Eleanor Jackson Piel first encountered Vincent Jenkins (later known as Warith Habib Abdal) in 1969, when she helped him appeal a homicide conviction. Despite losing, she always believed he was innocent. After Jenkins contacted her again in the early 1980s, while doing time for a rape in Buffalo he claimed he didn't commit, she started to take an interest in that case as well.

Piel's investigation turned up many holes in the prosecution's case. But it was not until several years later, when she read about the potential of DNA testing, that she wondered if the new technology might unlock any doors.

Years later, she determined that the rape kit linked to the crime contained a hair from the attacker. Piel spent $4,000 of her own money to have the hair tested, but the results were inconclusive.

After more time passed, she located another lab and arranged to have the state scientist send the evidence there, but Federal Express lost the kit. Luckily, the scientist had preserved another specimen, and Barry

Scheck of the Innocence Project spent $7,000 to have it sent to a better-equipped laboratory in Virginia.

After a complicated series of tests, the results excluded Abdal as the rapist. The Erie County district attorney fought to keep him in prison, but Abdal's lawyer sought a federal writ of habeas corpus, alleging that he was innocent and that further incarceration of an innocent man would violate the due process clause and Eighth Amendment prohibition against cruel and unusual punishment. U.S. district judge John T. Elfvin of the Western District of New York, who was in poor health, granted habeas corpus relief, and Abdal was freed after serving seventeen years in prison. Elfvin's action apparently represents the only known instance in which a federal judge has granted habeas corpus relief on a simple assertion of innocence (a bare innocence claim).

Monroe

An Ongoing Battle in Rochester

In September 1992, Frank Sterling was convicted of the murder of seventy-four-year-old Viola Manville in Hilton, Monroe County, three years earlier, based largely on his videotaped confession. During the trial his lawyer, Assistant Public Defender Thomas Kidera, argued that during a grueling, all-night interrogation, Sterling had entered into a hypnotic state that had induced him to parrot information provided to him by police investigators. But the jury voted to convict, and Sterling was sentenced to twenty-five years to life.

Four years later, stories began to surface about another local man, Mark Christie, who was then accused (and ultimately convicted) of the brutal bludgeoning murder of a four-year-old girl, Kali Ann Poulton. Newspaper accounts blamed Christie for Manville's murder. The implication was that if police and prosecutors had promptly apprehended Christie for the earlier slaying, Poulton's death might have been averted.

In response to mounting pressure, Monroe County district attorney Howard Relin agreed to a hearing on whether new evidence had been uncovered to warrant a retrial for Sterling. Eight persons testified that Christie had told them he had murdered Manville. But State Supreme Court Justice Donald Wisner ruled that the evidence in the case showed that Sterling, not Christie, had done the killing.

Sterling's lawyer, Donald Thompson, persisted. Before the Appellate Division, Fourth Department, he argued that prosecutors had illegally withheld evidence that helped prove Sterling did not commit the crime. But the appellate panel unanimously upheld Sterling's conviction.

In November 2000, Thompson called for genetic testing of a strand of hair found in the victim's left hand, saying it likely came from her attacker during their fierce struggle. Prosecutors countered that the hair could have come from anybody, including law enforcement investigators or lab technicians. But Thompson responded, "It's a long shot that the hair came from her assailant, but boy, if it did, it's going to be an uphill battle for Mr. Christie to explain how his hair ended up" in Manville's grasp.

As Thompson prepared to formally request that the county court allow a genetic comparison involving the hair evidence and DNA taken from Christie, his case posed a new question in the area of genetic testing jurisprudence. Although New York was one of only two states in the nation to legally give convicted felons the right to DNA testing to prove their innocence, the system was designed to allow inmates to ask for a match between their own DNA and crime scene evidence. Thompson, by contrast, was seeking to obtain a sample of Christie's DNA for comparison. Moreover, the testing in question would require a sample of Christie's monochondrial DNA—the genetic code found within hair strands and bones—as opposed to the nuclear DNA found in blood or saliva.

Although his lawyer claimed to have uncovered more new evidence raising questions about the police investigation of Manville and Christie, Sterling remained in prison, and the next step remained uncertain. Reporter Gary Craig continues to write stories about the case.

10

Selected Wrongful Conviction Cases

EVERETT APPLEGATE was convicted of murder in Nassau County in 1935, sentenced to death, and executed at Sing Sing on July 16, 1936. He was convicted based on the unsubstantiated testimony of his codefendant, who had previously been acquitted in two other murders. The prosecutor refused to support clemency for either defendant. Prison officials continued to assert that Applegate was innocent, and a number of scholarly studies have continued to list this case as a wrongful execution.

MIGUEL ARROYO was convicted of manslaughter in Kings County in 1965 for killing a boy who was fighting outside his store. The trial judge set aside the verdict after a series of eyewitnesses identified another man, Jose Valasquez, as the killer and key witnesses against Arroyo recanted their testimony. The indictment against Arroyo was dismissed, and Valasquez was indicted for murder.

THOMAS BAMBRICK was convicted of murder in 1915, sentenced to death, and executed. Prison authorities later discovered evidence that another convict had committed the crime. The case has continued to be listed by a number of scholarly studies as a wrongful execution.

JOSEPH BARBATO was convicted of first-degree murder in 1929 and sentenced to death. The conviction was reversed on the grounds that his four-word confession had been coerced by beating. Following a recommendation by the prosecutor, the trial judge ordered him released from prison in 1930.

ARTHUR BARBER was convicted of first-degree murder in Bronx County in 1969 and sentenced to life in prison. In 1975 a federal district court reversed the conviction on the grounds that Barber had been arrested without probable cause, beaten by the police, and subjected to numerous other violations of his constitutional rights. The court said his confession had been extracted by "brutal treatment." All charges were dismissed and he was released from prison, having served ten years.

LIEUTENANT CHARLES BECKER of the New York Police Department was convicted of murder in New York County in 1912 and legally executed at Sing Sing on July 30, 1915. Many insiders, including at least two Sing Sing wardens, insisted that Becker was innocent of the crime. The case continues to be listed in scholarly studies as a wrongful execution.

FERNANDO BERMUDEZ was convicted or murder in New York in 1991 and sentenced to twenty-three years to life. At this writing he is still in prison, awaiting action by a federal judge on his writ of habeas corpus.

TOM BIANCO was convicted of murder in Cayuga County in 1985. The conviction was vacated and the indictment dismissed in 1993, due to prosecutorial misconduct.

BRYAN BLAKE was convicted of second-degree in New York County in 1985 and sentenced to twenty-five years to life. Three years later, the conviction was reversed on the grounds that evidence shown to the jury had been unduly prejudicial.

JEFFREY BLAKE was convicted of a double murder in Kings County in 1991, based on perjured eyewitness testimony. The conviction was reversed and the charges were dropped in 1998.

LARRY BOONE was convicted of murder in Bronx County in 1973 and sentenced to twenty-five years to life. In 1975 the conviction was reversed because the prosecutor had failed to disclose crucial exculpatory evidence. On remand, the trial court dismissed all charges. In 1988 the Court of Claims granted Boone's summary judgment on his wrongful imprisonment claim. In March 1992 the Court of Claims awarded $45,000 to Robert S. Black, the administrator of his estate, Boone having died on March 26, 1991.

GEORGINA BORRERO a store security guard, was convicted of criminally negligent homicide in Bronx County in 1983. In 1986 the Appellate Division found that Borrero had acted "entirely reasonably" as a "responsible citizen" and had not broken any law. The conviction was reversed and the indictment dismissed.

CALVIN BOYETTE, who spent ten years in prison for setting a woman on fire, was freed in 2001 by an appellate court that accused the Brooklyn DA's office of suppressing exculpatory evidence.

LAMONT BRANCH was convicted in 1989 of murdering a drug dealer in Kings County and sentenced to twenty-five years to life. His family contended that the killer was his look-alike brother, Lorenzo Branch, who said he did the killing in self-defense. In 2002, after numerous hearings and extensive news coverage, Judge James Starkey overturned the conviction and Lorenzo Branch was freed after serving thirteen years behind bars.

LAZARO BURT was convicted of murder in Queens County in 1992, based on the testimony of a lone eyewitness, and spent ten years in prison before the conviction was overturned in state supreme court and another man was charged with the crime.

LEONARD CALLACE was convicted of sexual assault in 1987 in Suffolk County and sentenced to twenty-five to fifty years. In 1991 the conviction was reversed and the charges dismissed based on newly discovered DNA evidence.

BERTRAM CAMPBELL was convicted of forgery and served three years in prison before his conviction was thrown out, due to the discovery of various methods used by the police to identify him as the perpetrator. In 1948 the case was examined by the New York State Judicial Council.

JOSE CARRASQUILLO was convicted of second-degree manslaughter in New York County in 1986, after he and another person became involved in a fight with an alleged shoplifter in the boutique where he worked. Two years later, the Appellate Division reversed the conviction on the grounds that the evidence was insufficient to prove that Carrasquillo, rather than his accomplice, had inflicted the fatal blow.

NATHANIEL CARTER was convicted of murder in the stabbing of his mother-in-law in Queens County in 1982 and sentenced to twenty-five years to life. Carter was released after serving two and a half years in prison. In 1986 he received a settlement of $450,000 for his wrongful conviction and imprisonment.

Thomas A. Cenzi was convicted of second-degree murder in Monroe County in 1980 and sentenced to twenty-five years to life in prison. The Appellate Division ordered a new trial on the grounds that the trial judge had improperly allowed the jury to receive certain evidence. In 1983, Cenzi was acquitted of all charges.

Terry Leon Chalmers was convicted of rape, sodomy, robbery, and grand larceny in Westchester County in 1987 and sentenced to twelve to twenty-four years. In 1995 the conviction was reversed and the indictment dismissed, based on newly discovered DNA evidence.

William Chapman was convicted of arson in Albany County. The conviction was later overturned. In December 1993 he was awarded $50,000 by the Court of Claims.

Lambert Charles, age sixteen, pleaded guilty to manslaughter in Queens in 1993, after his identification in a police lineup and his own confession. Reinvestigation by the Queens district attorney led Supreme Court Justice Robert J. Hanophy to set aside the conviction.

Frank Cirofaci was convicted of murder in New York County in 1912 and legally executed at Sing Sing on April 13, 1914. Four other men were also executed for the crime. Two Sing Sing wardens stated they were convinced that Cirofaci had nothing to do with the crime.

Arthur Cleveland was convicted of murder (with Larry Boone) in Bronx County in 1973 and sentenced to twenty years to life in prison. The Appellate Division reversed the conviction in 1975 on the grounds that the prosecutor had unconstitutionally failed to disclose crucial exculpatory evidence. The second trial court dismissed all charges, and Cleveland was freed from prison after serving four and a half years. In 1991 he was awarded $57,011.85.

Marion Coakley was convicted of rape and robbery in Bronx County in 1983. He was released in 1987, based on newly discovered DNA evidence. In 1994 the Court of Claims awarded him $450,000.

Patricia Cohen was convicted of second-degree murder in Westchester County in 1979 and sentenced to twenty years to life. She insisted her husband had committed suicide. After she made an unsuccessful appeal to the Appellate Division, the Court of Appeals reversed and vacated the conviction, based on ballistics evidence. On remand, the trial court suppressed certain evidence and the prosecutor unsuccessfully appealed all the way to the U.S. Supreme Court. Cohen was ultimately convicted only of criminal possession of a weapon in the third degree.

TIMOTHY CROSBY was convicted of second-degree assault and criminal possession of a weapon in Kings County in 1988, based on perjured testimony. The conviction was reversed and the charges were dropped in 1999.

RAFAEL CRUZ was convicted of murder in Kings County in 1976. The Appellate Division reversed on the grounds that Cruz had been improperly questioned, ordered the statement in question suppressed, and remanded for a new trial. In the retrial, he was acquitted of all charges.

CHARLES DABBS was convicted of first-degree rape in Westchester County in 1984 and sentenced to twelve and a half to twenty years. In 1991 the conviction was reversed and the indictment dismissed, based on newly discovered DNA evidence.

CHARLES DANIELS was convicted of sexual assault and murder of a child in Queens and subjected to extreme abuse by staff and inmates in prison. He was later exonerated.

EDWARD DENNIS was convicted in 1937 in Rensselaer County of unlawful entry and petit larceny and sentenced to a term of six months, after his guilty plea. Governor Herbert Lehman granted clemency in 1937 following recommendations of the district attorney and the sentencing judge that he was innocent.

MELVIN DLUGASH was convicted of murder in Kings County in 1975. Dlugash appealed on the grounds that he had fired at the victim after the victim was already dead, in order to avoid being harmed by the killer. The Appellate Division set aside the murder conviction, substituted a verdict of attempted murder, and remanded the case for resentencing.

JOHN DUVAL was convicted of second-degree murder in Monroe County in 1973 and sentenced to twenty-five years. Duval's conviction was overturned in 1999 and he was acquitted.

VERNON ELLIS was convicted of first-degree manslaughter in New York County in 1976. The Appellate Division set aside the conviction on the grounds that the judge had acted like a prosecutor rather than as an independent arbiter. The prosecutor dropped all charges, and Ellis was freed after serving two years on the wrongful conviction.

REINALDO ESTRADA was convicted of several counts of murder in Bronx County in 1986 and sentenced to twenty-five years to life on each count. Two years later the Appellate Division found several instances of prosecutorial misconduct and reversed. Estrada was later retried and acquitted of all charges.

CHARLES EVERETT was convicted of first-degree murder in 1960 and sentenced to life. After the conviction was affirmed on appeal, a federal circuit court found that "Everett was arrested illegally, held incommunicado and questioned extensively without counsel or warning of his right to counsel or his right to remain silent, and the confession followed upon deception and false promises of assistance if he should confess." After the prosecution failed to retry him, the indictment was dismissed, and he was released after serving four years in prison.

ANTHONY FAISON was convicted of murder in Kings County in 1987. The conviction was reversed in 2001, and he was released after it was shown that the sole eyewitness against him had lied in order to collect a reward.

FRANCIS FEATHERSTONE was convicted of murder in New York County in 1986, for allegedly killing an associate of the "Westies" gang. Prosecutors later conceded that Featherstone had not been at the scene and that he had been framed by the killer. Postconviction investigation also revealed that Featherstone's trial lawyer had concealed the fact that another of his clients had confessed to the murder. The trial court subsequently dismissed all charges against Featherstone, based on newly discovered evidence, and he was freed after being wrongfully imprisoned for a year and a half.

TERRENCE FERRER was convicted of murder in Bronx County in 1974 and sentenced to fifteen years to life. His two codefendants were convicted of manslaughter and sentenced to prison for up to seven years. The Appellate Division vacated his conviction and remanded for a new trial because he had not been advised that his trial attorney had a potential conflict of interest by representing all three codefendants. Ferrer was later retried and acquitted of all charges.

ALFIO FERRO was convicted of second-degree murder in Queens County in 1977. After the Appellate Division upheld his conviction, the Court of Appeals reversed and ordered a new trial, on the grounds that the police had wrongfully induced him to speak after he had invoked his right to remain silent. After remand for a second trial, Ferro pleaded guilty to robbery in exchange for a sentence of time served.

WILLIAM FISHER was convicted of first-degree manslaughter in 1933 and sentenced to fifteen to thirty years. In 1944 he was paroled. In 1958 the judgment of conviction was vacated when it was shown that the prosecutor had fabricated gun evidence against him and suppressed exculpatory evidence that clearly demonstrated his innocence. Six legislative bills to compensate him for his ordeal were vetoed, until one such was signed by Governor Mario Cuomo in 1984.

ELVERTON FREELAND was convicted of murder and attempted murder in Erie County in 1973 and sentenced to twenty years to life, based on the testimony of a single eyewitness. The trial judge rebuffed defense's efforts to introduce evidence bearing on the credibility of the witness, who was a heroin addict. After the Appellate Division affirmed the conviction, the Court of Appeals reversed, and the eyewitness later recanted her identification. After the district attorney moved for the dismissal of all charges against Freeland, he was released from prison in 1977.

RUBEN GARSON was convicted of second-degree murder in Queens County in 1983 and sentenced to twenty years to life. The Appellate Division overturned his conviction on the grounds that the trial judge had mistakenly charged the jury, and the matter was remanded for a new trial. This time Garson was acquitted.

JOSEPH GIULIANO was convicted of first-degree manslaughter in Bronx County in 1983 and sentenced to six to eighteen years. After the Appellate Division affirmed his conviction, the Court of Appeals ordered the indictment dismissed on the grounds that the circumstantial evidence presented was insufficient to prove guilt beyond a reasonable doubt, and Giuliano was freed after serving two years.

HECTOR GONZALEZ was arrested for stabbing a man and slitting his throat during a gang fight outside a Brooklyn nightclub in 1995, based on an eyewitness's identification. Convicted of second-degree murder in

Kings County, he was sentenced to fifteen years to life. In April 2002 he was released from prison shortly after DNA test results cleared him of the crime and a criminal court judge approved the DA's motion to throw out the murder conviction and vacate the sentence.

ROBERT GRIMALDI was convicted of murder in Queens County in 1973, based on the testimony of an eyewitness. The Appellate Division reversed the conviction and dismissed the indictment as based on insufficient evidence, ruling that the testimony did not support the conclusion that Grimaldi was guilty of murder.

STEPHEN GRZECHOWIAK was convicted of felony murder in Erie County in 1929, sentenced to death, and legally executed at Sing Sing on July 17, 1930. A codefendant insisted that Grzechowiak was not involved in the crime and claimed that the eyewitness was mistaken.

ROY HALE was convicted of second-degree murder in Queens County in 1984 and sentenced to twenty years to life. The Appellate Division reversed the conviction and dismissed the indictment as based on insufficient evidence. Hale was released after having served three and one-half years.

CHARLES HAMILTON was convicted of second-degree murder and first-degree robbery in Suffolk County in 1982, and sentenced to twenty-five years to life, at the age of nineteen. At this writing, he is still in prison.

NGUYEN HOC (a.k.a. **HOC THAI VU**) was convicted of second-degree murder in New York in 1986 and sentenced to fifteen years to life. In July 1991 the State Court of Claims awarded him $188,515.31 for wrongful conviction and imprisonment.

HARRY L. HOFFMAN was convicted of second-degree murder in 1924 and sentenced to twenty years to life. On appeal the conviction was reversed, due to faulty wording of the indictment. A second trial ended in a mistrial after the defense attorney collapsed from a heart attack. The third trial resulted in a hung jury. At the fourth trial in 1929, testimony was presented that the original eyewitness had committed perjury and the fatal shots could not have come from Hoffman's gun, and Hoffman was acquitted.

LOUIS HOFFNER was convicted of first-degree murder in 1941 and sentenced to life. A newspaper reporter later proved his innocence and revealed extensive misconduct by police and prosecutors. Hoffner was released and later awarded damages for wrongful conviction and imprisonment.

L. L. Ivey Jr. was convicted of three counts of murder in Erie County in 1976 and sentenced to twenty-five years to life. The Appellate Division reversed the conviction, citing extensive prosecutorial misconduct. At his retrial, Ivey presented a strong alibi defense and presented another witness who implicated another person in the murder. Ivey was acquitted of all charges and released after having served five and one-half years. In 1990 the Court of Claims granted summary judgment on his suit for wrongful conviction and imprisonment.

Andre Jackson was convicted of murder and possession of a weapon in Kings County in 1987 and sentenced to fifteen years to life. In December 1991 he was awarded $302,100 by the Court of Claims.

Edmond D. Jackson was convicted of murder and felony murder in Queens County in 1972 and sentenced to two concurrent terms of twenty years to life. The convictions were affirmed on appeal. In 1978 a petition for habeas corpus in federal court resulted in a reversal of the conviction on the grounds of unreliable witness testimony and the fact that no other evidence had linked him to the crime. The U.S. Court of Appeals upheld the ruling and further criticized the district attorney for proceeding with the charges based on insufficient evidence and ignoring other evidence that pointed to another suspect.

Erick Jackson was convicted of arson and six counts of murder in Kings County in 1978, for the deaths of six New York City firefighters who perished in a blaze at a supermarket. The trial judge later found that the district attorney had withheld crucial evidence from the defense, pointing toward a cause of faulty electrical wiring and arson by the fire investigators. The conviction was vacated and Jackson was released in 1988, after serving ten years in prison.

Patsy Kelly Jarrett was convicted of second-degree murder and first-degree robbery in Oneida County in 1977 and sentenced to twenty-five years to life. In 1986, after nine years in custody, her petition for a writ of habeas corpus was granted by U.S. district judge David Edelstein of the Southern District, on the grounds that the identification at trial was the product of an unduly suggestive photographic identification procedure and had no independent basis. Although offered a sentence of time served in exchange for a guilty plea, she refused to plead guilty because she was innocent, and the state later won its appeal, resulting in her continued confinement. She is still in prison.

VICTOR JENKINS (a.k.a. **WARITH HABIB ABDAL**), convicted of raping a Buffalo woman in 1982, served seventeen years in New York state prisons before DNA proved he was not the rapist. He was exonerated in 1999.

MELVIN JOHNSON was convicted of felony murder in Orleans County in 1982 and sentenced to twenty years to life. His appeals lawyer argued that his assigned public defender had put up an inadequate defense, and the trial court granted the motion. On retrial he was acquitted of all charges.

ROBERT JOHNSON was convicted of forgery in Westchester County in 1980 and sentenced to thirty months to five years. The Appellate Division reversed the conviction in 1982 on the grounds of insufficient evidence. In June 1982 the Court of Claims awarded $52,590 to his estate.

THOMAS KAPATOS was convicted of second-degree murder in 1938 and sentenced to twenty years to life. In 1962 a federal judge overturned the conviction on the ground that the prosecutor had prejudiced the case by suppressing exculpatory evidence from an eyewitness.

AHMAD KASSIM was convicted of first-degree manslaughter in 1958 and sentenced to five to ten years. In 1965 his conviction was vacated on the ground that the confession had been illegally obtained and had arisen from poor translation. Another person had also confessed to the crime. The indictment was dismissed, and Kassim was released after serving seven years. Efforts to enact legislation that would enable him to recover damages from the state were finally successful in 1984.

JOSEPH A. KLEMM was convicted of murder in Dutchess County in 1984 and sentenced to twenty-five years to life. The Appellate Division overturned the conviction and sentence on the grounds that the trial court had failed to properly instruct the jury. On retrial, Klemm was acquitted of all charges and released after serving four years. In 1988 the Court of Claims granted summary judgment on his claim for unjust conviction and imprisonment.

DAVID KNATZ was convicted of first-degree manslaughter in Queens County in 1978 and sentenced to twelve and a half to twenty-five years. The Appellate Division reversed the conviction, ruling it was based largely on statements he was overheard to have made while talking in his sleep. On remand, Knatz pleaded guilty to attempted assault in the first degree, and he was resentenced to three to six years.

KERRY KOTLER was convicted of rape in Suffolk County in 1981 and sentenced to twenty-five to fifty years. The conviction was reversed and the charges dismissed in 1992. On June 30, 1997, he received $1,510,000 from the Court of Claims.

CHARLES LAMBERT at age sixteen was convicted of manslaughter in 1993 after confessing and pleading guilty in Queens. He was later exonerated by the Queens DA.

EDWARD LARKMAN was convicted of murder in 1925 and sentenced to death, based on mistaken eyewitness identification. Ten hours before his scheduled execution, his sentence was commuted to life imprisonment by Governor Al Smith. In 1929 another convict confessed to the crime, and in 1933, Governor Herbert Lehman issued an unconditional pardon and set him free.

LESTER LEE was convicted of murder in Kings County in 1973 after the first trial resulted in a hung jury. He was sentenced to twenty-five years to life. After the Appellate Division reversed the conviction and vacated the sentence, two retrials failed to produce a unanimous verdict. Finally, in 1977, the trial court dismissed the charges and Lee was released.

SAMI LEKA, an Albanian Muslim, was convicted of murder in Kings County in 1990, based on the testimony of two eyewitnesses. A CBS news producer obtained information about the case and told it to a lawyer who was a former federal prosecutor, and although the producer's story never aired, the lawyer took on the case. Afer Leka has spent eleven years behind bars, the U.S. Court of Appeals for the Second Circuit reversed the conviction and ordered a new trial, ruling that Brooklyn prosecutors "for a critical time actively suppressed" key evidence in the case—the report that an off-duty police officer had witnessed the shooting and provided a different version of the crime. Leka walked out of jail eight days later.

CAMILO LEYRA was convicted of murdering his parents in 1950 and sentenced to death. On appeal his conviction was reversed, on the ground that his confession was coerced. Two more times he was retried and convicted, but his conviction was reversed, based on his confession. Finally the court ordered the indictment dismissed and sharply criticized the prosecution for relying exclusively on a confession. Leyra was released after serving five years in the death house.

LEE LONG was convicted of rape in Queens and sentenced to eight to fifteen years. He served six years before being exonerated in June 2000. Legal Aid lawyers Susan Epstein and Seymour James helped get his case reinvestigated by Gregory Lasak, working with two retired police homicide investigators.

CAMILO LOPEZ was convicted of murder in New York County in 1985 and sentenced to twenty years to life. After the Appellate Division upheld the conviction, the Court of Appeals reversed the conviction and ordered a new trial, on the grounds that the trial judge had improperly referred to inadmissible evidence. On retrial, Lopez was acquitted.

LUIS MARIN was convicted of twenty-six counts of murder in Westchester County, following a 1980 hotel fire. The trial court dismissed the indictments based on insufficiency of the trial evidence, and the prosecution appealed. The dismissal was upheld by the Appellate Division and the Court of Appeals, which ruled in 1984 that Marin's criminal responsibility for the fire had not been proven.

ANGELO MARTINEZ was convicted of murder in Queens County and sentenced to twenty-five years to life in 1986. While in prison in 1992 he was convicted of a federal drug offense. However, in 2002 his murder conviction was overturned and the charge dismissed by a Queens judge after prosecutors acknowledged that a contract killer had confessed to the crime in 1989 and that his confession had been supported by a polygraph test. Federal authorities later agreed to release him on time served for the drug offense.

LUCIUS MASON was convicted of second-degree murder in New York County in 1984 and sentenced to twenty years to life. A later, unrelated federal trial produced evidence that other persons had committed the murder. The district attorney joined in the motion by defense to dismiss all charges against Mason. In 1988 he was released, after having served five and one-half years.

PIETRO MATERA was convicted of first-degree murder in 1931 and sentenced to death. After the conviction was affirmed, Governor Franklin D. Roosevelt commuted the sentence to life. In 1960 the real culprit's wife confessed on her deathbed that she had fingered Matera to save her husband. Matera was released from prison in 1961.

KENNETH MAULA was convicted of first-degree manslaughter in Bronx County in 1987 and sentenced to six to eighteen years. The Appellate Division reversed the conviction and ordered a retrial based on the grounds that the trial court had failed to properly instruct the jury. On retrial, Maula was acquitted of manslaughter and convicted of only a weapons charge.

WILLIAM A. MAYNARD was convicted of first-degree manslaughter in New York County in 1971, after two previous trials had ended with hung juries. He was sentenced to ten to twenty years. The Appellate Division affirmed the conviction, but in 1974 the state supreme court, with concurrence from the district attorney, dismissed all charges on finding that the prosecution had suppressed evidence about the unreliability of the chief witness, who had a long history of psychiatric hospitalization. Maynard was released, having served six and a half years in prison.

EMEL MCDOWELL was convicted of second-degree murder in Kings County in 1992 and sentenced to twenty-two years to life. At this writing he is still in prison.

ROBERT MCLAUGHLIN was convicted of second-degree murder in Kings County in 1981 and sentenced to fifteen years to life. In 1986 the district attorney admitted that his conviction was erroneous and joined in defense's motion to dismiss the charges. McLaughlin was released after having served six years on his wrongful conviction. In 1989 he was awarded $1,940,805 by the Court of Claims.

EFREN MERALLA was convicted of a double homicide in New York County in 1990 and sentenced to twenty-five years to life. The conviction was later reversed on grounds of ineffective counsel and judgment was vacated in 1994.

RUBEN MONTALVO was convicted of second-degree murder in New York County in 1989 and sentenced to fifteen years to life. In 2001 a federal judge reversed the conviction and ordered him released, after rebuking the prosecution for a lack of evidence.

JOSE MORALES was convicted of second-degree murder in New York in 1989 and sentenced to fifteen years to life. In 2001 a federal judge reversed his conviction and ordered him released, after rebuking the prosecution for a lack of evidence.

ANGEL NIEVES was convicted of second-degree manslaughter in Bronx County in 1982 and sentenced to four to eight years. The Court of Appeals reversed the conviction and dismissed the indictment on the grounds that the evidence consisted of unreliable and inadmissible statements. After the prosecutor did not pursue a new indictment, Nieves was released, having served four years.

ANTONIO NIEVES was convicted of second-degree murder and other offenses in Queens County in 1984 and sentenced to twenty-five years to life. The Appellate Division reversed the conviction and dismissed the charges on the ground of insufficient evidence. Nieves was released after having served six years.

JULIO NIEVES was convicted in Kings County. In July 1993 the State Court of Claims awarded him $222,833.97 for wrongful conviction and imprisonment.

JIM O'DONNELL was convicted of assault and robbery in New York County and sentenced to two and one-third to seven years. The conviction was reversed on appeal in December 2000, after he had served three years in prison, when DNA tests arranged by his Legal Aid lawyer Lori Shellenberger showed he was not the attacker.

RUBIN ORTEGA was convicted of murder in the second degree and criminal possession of a weapon in the second degree in Kings County in 1991, based on the testimony of an eyewitness who was found to have perjured himself to convict defendants in at least two other cases. In 2003 the U.S. Court of Appeals for the Second Circuit threw out his conviction and ordered a new trial.

VICTOR ORTIZ was convicted of felonious rape and sodomy in Orange County in 1984. He was released in October 1996 after newly discovered DNA evidence resulted in the overturning of his conviction. In

June 1997 he received a total of $560,905.96 from the Court of Claims.

PAUL PALMER was convicted of second-degree murder in Rensselaer County in 1984. The Appellate Division reversed the conviction and ordered a new trial because the prosecutor had suppressed exculpatory evidence. In 1988, Palmer was acquitted of homicide and convicted of robbery and burglary.

RICHARD PARIS was convicted of criminally negligent homicide in Kings County in 1986 and sentenced to one to three years. Two years later the Appellate Division reversed the conviction and dismissed the charge on the grounds that the evidence was insufficient to support the charge.

KENNETH G. PAVEL was convicted of sexual assault in Onondaga County in 1989 and sentenced to two consecutive terms of four to twelve years. He was paroled in 1998, but reincarcerated because he continued to refuse to admit his guilt. In 2001 the U.S. Court of Appeals in the Second Circuit overturned his conviction ruling that his lawyer had failed to put up an effective defense. The Onondaga DA later decided to drop further prosecution.

PAUL PFEFFER was convicted of second-degree murder in 1954 and sentenced to twenty years to life. He claimed he was innocent and said his confession had been coerced by the police. Another man, John Roche, was later arrested, and he confessed to the murder, prompting police to reopen the investigation. After Pfeffer passed a series of lie detector tests, he was granted a new trial. After he had been reindicted for first-degree manslaughter and was awaiting trial, he was indicted and tried in another case, for which he was convicted of second-degree murder and sentenced to twenty years to life. The manslaughter charge in the first case was dropped. Roche, meanwhile, was never tried for the murder for which Pfeffer was originally convicted, but he was convicted and executed for another killing.

RENE PICCARRETO was convicted of homicide in Monroe County in 1978. He was released after it was discovered that the prosecution had used false evidence and perjured testimony to obtain the conviction.

DIOMEDES POLONIA was convicted of attempted murder in Bronx County in 1998, based on an identification made by the shooting victim who was under medication, even though Polonia had provided an alibi to his attorney, which his attorney had never checked out. The trial attorney did not call the defendant's witness to support the alibi. Polonia later obtained *pro bono* assistance from Davis, Polk & Wardwell, who were overseen by the Criminal Appeals Bureau of the Legal Aid Society. In 2003 the conviction was thrown out in Bronx Supreme Court. Judge Peter J. Benitez ruled that counsel had been ineffective at trial and the Bronx DA chose not to retry the case.

JAMES PRIESTER was convicted of first-degree manslaughter in Rensselaer County in 1979. The Appellate Division reversed the conviction on the grounds of prosecutorial and judicial misconduct. In 1984, Priester was retried and acquitted of all charges.

PETER QUARTARARO was convicted of two counts of second-degree murder in Suffolk County in 1981 and sentenced to two concurrent terms of nine years to life. The U.S. District Court granted a writ of habeas corpus and ordered the suppression of information that the police had obtained after unlawfully failing to advise Quartararo of his rights. The writ and suppression order were upheld by the Second Circuit Court of Appeals. In 1989 the prosecution dismissed all charges.

ALBERT RAMOS was convicted of sexual abuse involving a child in Bronx County in 1985 and sentenced to eight and a third to twenty-five years. In 1994 the conviction was reversed and the charges were dismissed, after it was shown that the child had fabricated a prior claim of sexual abuse and that city officials and the district attorney had failed to disclose exculpatory evidence.

ANGEL RAMOS was convicted of second-degree murder in New York County in 1983 and sentenced to twenty-five years to life. The Appellate Division reversed the conviction after the prosecutor conceded that the judge's instructions to the jury had misstated the law. On retrial, Ramos was acquitted and released.

WALLACE REDMAN was convicted of second-degree murder in Oswego County in 1980 and sentenced to fifteen years to life. The Appellate Division reversed the conviction on the grounds that evidence used against him had been illegally obtained, and it ordered a new trial. After no further charges were brought, Redman was released, having served nearly six years.

GREGORY REED was convicted of murder in Kings County in 1979 and sentenced to fifteen years to life. The Court of Appeals overturned the conviction in 1985 on the grounds that the testimony of the sole witness contained important contradictions. In 1989, Reed was awarded $495,000 by the Court of Claims for unjust conviction and imprisonment.

MARY REED was convicted of first-degree manslaughter in Westchester County in 1973, based on the testimony of a single eyewitness. After the Appellate Division confirmed the conviction, the Court of Appeals reversed the conviction and dismissed all charges on the grounds that the witness was not credible.

VINCENT RIVERS was convicted of second-degree murder on retrial in Kings County in 1983, following an Appellate Division reversal of his conviction in a previous trial. A third trial ended in a mistrial. His conviction at a fourth trial was reversed because of numerous prejudicial errors by the trial court. At a fifth trial, he was acquitted on all counts.

LUIS KEVIN ROJAS was convicted of murder in Greenwich Village in 1990, when he was eighteen, and later acquitted in October 1998, after serving half of his fifteen-years-to-life sentence.

SAMUEL RUSSOTI was convicted of murder in Monroe County in 1978. Subsequent to the conviction, it was revealed that prosecutors and sheriff's deputies had knowingly used false evidence and perjured testimony to obtain the conviction. The district attorney consented to vacate the convictions and dismiss the homicide charges.

MAX RYBARCZYK was convicted of felony murder in Erie County in 1929, sentenced to death, and legally executed at Sing Sing on July 17, 1930. A codefendant insisted that Rybarczyk was not involved in the crime and claimed that the eyewitness was mistaken.

KERRY SANDERS was arrested in October 1993 in Los Angeles and imprisoned at Greenhaven Correctional Facility. He was released in 1995 when it was established that he should never have been arrested, having been mistaken for Robert Sanders. After the case was highlighted in the *New York Times Magazine* in August 2000, Kerry Sanders received a settlement of $3.2 million.

CHARLES SBERNA was convicted of murder in New York County in 1938, sentenced to death, and legally executed at Sing Sing on January 5, 1939. His codefendant insisted Sberna was innocent. Later it was discovered that the same police official who had made the case against him had also been involved in the miscarriage of justice against Isidore Zimmerman. Sberna's case is listed in scholarly studies as a wrongful execution.

CHARLES SHEPARD was convicted of murder in Kings County. In 2001 the conviction was reversed and the charges were dropped, after it was shown that the sole eyewitness against him had lied to collect a reward.

LAWRENCE SOLOMON was convicted of criminal sale of a controlled substance in Bronx County in 1977 and sentenced to six years to life. His conviction was later thrown out. In April 1992 the Court of Claims awarded him $187,050 for his wrongful conviction and imprisonment.

FRANK STERLING was convicted of second-degree murder in Monroe County in 1992 and sentenced to twenty-five years to life. At this writing he is still in prison.

ARTHUR STEWART was convicted of first-degree burglary and second-degree robbery in Queens in 1995 and sentenced to seven to fourteen years, based on statements by two eyewitnesses who testified against their longtime acquaintance. In July 2001 he was released from Mid-Orange Correctional Facility, after a *pro se* writ of habeas corpus prompted Eastern District judge Edward Korman to appoint two top attorneys to look into the case. Following a reinvestigation by the Queens DA that included polygraph tests, the DA moved to vacate the conviction.

DWAYNE SUTTON was convicted of two counts of second-degree murder in Kings County in 1984 and sentenced to twenty years to life. The Appellate Division reversed the convictions and ordered a new trial on the basis that the court had improperly instructed the jury. In 1987, after a retrial, Sutton was acquitted and released.

MARTIN TANKLEFF was convicted of murdering his parents in Suffolk County and sentenced to two consecutive terms of twenty-five years to life. At this writing he is still in prison.

SAMMY THOMAS was convicted of second-degree murder in Cayuga County in 1978 and sentenced to fifteen years to life. During the appeal, the prosecutor discovered that the original prosecutor had illegally withheld extensive exculpatory evidence. The Appellate Division reversed the conviction and ordered a new trial. The charges against Thomas were dismissed on motion.

WILLIE GENE THOMAS was convicted of murder in Cayuga County in 1978. The Appellate Division reversed the conviction on the grounds that the prosecution had withheld exculpatory evidence. He was acquitted at the retrial.

RICARDO TORRES was convicted of murder in Kings County in 1987. The Appellate Division reversed the conviction and dismissed the indictment, holding that the prosecution had failed to prove its case.

BETTY TYSON spent more than twenty-five years in prison before her murder conviction in Rochester was overturned and the City of Rochester awarded her damages.

JOHN VALLETUTI was convicted of first-degree murder in 1947 and sentenced to death, over the jury's recommendation of life imprisonment. The conviction was reversed on appeal because his confession had been obtained by unlawful beating and testimony against him had also been obtained by physical coercion. The prosecutor supported the dismissal of the indictment, and Valletuti was released after having served two years in prison.

COLLINS (COLIN) HILLARY WARNER was convicted of second-degree murder in Kings County in 1982, based on testimony by child witnesses. He was sentenced to fifteen years to life. In 2001, Judge John Leventhal reversed the conviction. After conducting a reinvestigation and administering polygraph tests to the witnesses, the DA did not oppose Warner's release.

MICHAEL WASHINGTON was convicted of murder in Kings County in 1988, after a mistrial. The Appellate Division reversed the conviction and dismissed the indictment, holding that there was insufficient evidence against Washington.

ERNEST WELCOME was convicted of murder in Bronx County in 1970 and sentenced to two concurrent terms of twenty-five years to life. After an unsuccessful appeal, he asked the trial court to set aside the convictions on the ground that a key prosecution witness had recanted and admitted committing perjury. After denial of this petition, he commenced a federal habeas corpus proceeding but lost, then appealed to the Second Circuit Court of Appeals. In 1977 that court directed the writ be granted, and Welcome was retried. After his acquittal, he was set free, having served seven years.

SAMUEL TITO WILLIAMS was convicted of first-degree murder in 1947 and sentenced to death, despite the jury's recommendation of life. On appeal, the conviction was reversed on the ground that his confession had been coerced. He later recovered damages from the state for malicious prosecution.

GEORGE CHEW WING was convicted of first-degree murder in New York County in 1937, sentenced to death, and legally executed at Sing Sing on June 10, 1937. Wing convinced prison authorities that he had been falsely identified by eyewitnesses and victimized by perjured testimony.

RANDOLPH WOODHULL was convicted of second-degree murder in Kings County in 1982 and sentenced to twenty-five years to life. The Appellate Division reversed the conviction, holding that the prosecutor had made prejudicial statements at trial, and a new trial was ordered. He was acquitted and freed after serving three years.

ISIDORE ZIMMERMAN was convicted of first-degree murder in 1937 and sentenced to death. His conviction was affirmed although the Appeals Court acknowledged that he had not been at the scene of the crime. Within an hour of his scheduled execution, Governor Herbert Lehman commuted his sentence to life. But after twenty-four years in prison, the conviction was reversed, a new trial was ordered, the indictment was dismissed, and Zimmerman was released. In 1982 the Court of Claims agreed that the prosecutor had known that Zimmerman was innocent and had suppressed evidence and intimidated witnesses into committing perjury. In 1983, Zimmerman was awarded $1 million, but he died four months later.

Appendix

Brooklyn Law School
Second Look Program
Questionnaire

Name   Dept. Ident. # (DIN)
Mailing Address

   I. Basic Information About You and Your Case

   1. Please provide the county and indictment number (including year) of your case.
   2. What crimes were you indicted for?
   3. What crimes were you convicted of?
   4. Did your case go to trial or did you plead guilty?
   5. On what date were you sentenced?
   6. What is your sentence?
   7. Do you currently have an attorney?
   8. If you do currently have an attorney, please list his/her name, address, and telephone number.
   9. What is your date of birth?
   10. What was the highest grade that you completed in school?
   11. Other than your current conviction, have you ever been convicted of any other crimes?
If you have any prior convictions, please state (a) what they were for, and (b) when and where they were prosecuted, and (c) what sentences were imposed.

II. Trial. If your case went to trial, please answer the following questions. If you *pled guilty* before trial, please go to *Question #5* of this section.

1. Background
    a. Did you give a statement/confession to law enforcement officials in this case? Yes or no? If "yes," then what were the contents of that statement/confession and why did you give it?
    b. Were there any pre-trial motions and hearings in your case (such as motions to suppress statements to the police or physical evidence)? Yes or no? If "yes," then what were they?
    c. Who was your attorney at trial (include name, address, telephone number)?
    d. Who was the prosecuting attorney (Assistant District Attorney)?
    e. Who was the judge who presided at your trial?
    f. What was your defense at trial?
2. Testimony
    a. Who testified *against you* at trial?
    b. If the prosecution called expert witnesses (example: doctor, handwriting expert, etc.), who were they and what did they testify about?
    c. Did you testify in your own defense? Yes or no? If "No," why didn't you testify?
    d. Did any other witnesses testify on your behalf? Yes or no? If "yes," please indicate who they were and what they testified about.
3. Identifications
    a. Did any victim identify you? Yes or no? If "yes," then when and where (example: at the scene of the crime, during a lineup, in court, elsewhere)?
    b. Did anyone else identify you? Yes or no? If "yes," who identified you and when and where did the identification take place? Did that person testify at your trial? Yes or no?
4. Other Evidence
    a. Was any physical or biological evidence recovered during the investigation of your case? Yes or no? If "yes," then please indicate what evidence was found:
    i. *From You:*
        1. Hair sample
        2. Saliva
        3. Blood
        4. Semen
        5. Fingerprints
    ii. *From Any Victim:*
        1. Hair sample
        2. Saliva
        3. Blood
        4. Semen

b. Was any testing done on bodily fluids or hair samples? Yes or no? If "yes," then what kind of testing was done and who arranged for the testing (the prosecution or your attorney)?

c. Were the results of any tests used at trial? Yes or no? If "no," why not?

5. Guilty Pleas (Please answer only if you pled guilty.)
   a. Did your attorney talk to you about the plea agreement? Yes or no?
   b. Did you want to plead guilty or did you want to go to trial?
   c. If you wanted to go to trial, why did you plead guilty?

III. Appeal

1. If you filed an appeal with the Appellate Division, when did that court issue its decision?
2. Who was the attorney who handled your appeal (include name, address, and telephone number)?
3. What legal arguments were presented in that appeal?
4. Did you or your attorney file an application with the New York Court of Appeals to hear your case? Yes or no? If "yes," then:
   a. Did the Court of Appeals accept the case for review? Yes or no? If "yes," then when did that court decide the case?
   b. If the Court of Appeals did not accept your case for review, on what date did it deny your application?
   c. Have you begun any other post-conviction proceedings in your case (440 motions in state court or federal habeas corpus petitions)? Yes or no? If "yes," then
      i. What are they and in which court did you begin those proceedings?
      ii. Has that court made any decision? Yes or no? If "yes," then when did that court make the decision and what did that court decide?
      iii. Who was the attorney who handled your post-conviction proceedings, if any (name, address, telephone number)?

IV. Basis of Innocence Claim

1. In your current case, is there any evidence that was not known at the time of your conviction that could now help to prove your innocence? Yes or no? If "yes," then please describe the new evidence and explain why it was not considered at trial.
2. Is this new evidence available to you? Yes or no? If presenting the new evidence would involve the testimony of witnesses, why do you think the witnesses will come forward on your behalf?

V. Case Materials: Check (X) those documents below that you can make available to us. Please do not send any materials to us unless we specifically request them.

If you have already sent us certain materials, please indicate below which materials you have sent (X sent).

1. Hearing Transcript(s)
2. Trial Transcript
3. Police Report(s) (please describe)
4. Laboratory Report(s) (please describe)
5. Appellate Briefs
   Appellant (defense)
   Respondent (prosecution)
6. Post-Conviction Motion Papers and Memoranda of Law
   Defense
   Prosecution
7. Court Opinions

This is the end of the Second Look Program Questionnaire.
Please check to make sure that you have fully answered all of the questions that apply to your case. Please return the completed questionnaire to Professor William E. Hellerstein, Second Look Program, Brooklyn Law School, 250 Joralemon Street, Brooklyn, NY 11201.

Reprinted by permission of William Hellerstein, Second Look Program, Brooklyn Law School, 250 Joralemon St., Brooklyn, NY 11201

Selected References

Avenoso, Karen. 1997. "The Defense Never Rests." *Boston Globe Magazine*, February 2, 3–16.

Barber, Peter G. 1985. "Note: *People v. Smith*: Mandatory Death Laid to Rest." *Albany Law Review* 49(4) (Summer): 926–66.

Barnouw, Erik. 1996. "Bud Leyra." In *Media Marathon: A Twentieth-Century Memoir*. Durham, NC: Duke University Press.

Bedau, Hugo Adam, and Michael L. Radelet. 1987. "Miscarriages of Justice in Potentially Capital Cases." *Stanford Law Review* 40 (November): 21–179.

———. 1988. "The Myth of Infallibility: A Reply to Markman and Cassell." *Stanford Law Review* 41 (November): 161–70.

Bernhard, Adele. 1999. "When Justice Fails: Indemnification for Unjust Conviction." *University of Chicago Law School Roundtable* 6: 73.

Borchard, Edwin M. 1932. *Convicting the Innocent: Sixty-five Actual Errors of Criminal Justice*. New Haven, CT: Yale University Press.

Brandon, Ruth, and Christie Davies. 1973. *Wrongful Imprisonment: Mistaken Convictions and Their Consequences*. Hamden, CT: Archon Books.

Brandon, Stuart K. 1949. "To the Rescue of Charlie Stielow." *Reader's Digest*, April, 73–78.

Cleary, James. 1997. "When the Prisoner Is Innocent." *Human Rights* 14 (Spring): 42.

Coffee, John C. Jr. 1981. *Twisting Slowly in the Wind*. Chicago: University of Chicago Press.

Cole, Simon A. 2001. *Suspect Identities: A History of Fingerprinting and Criminal Identification*. Cambridge, MA: Harvard University Press.

Conners, Edward. 1996. *Convicted by Juries, Exonerated by Science: Case Studies in the Use of DNA Evidence to Establish Innocence after Trial*. Washington, DC: U.S. Department of Justice.

Connery, David S., ed. 1996. *Convicting the Innocent*. Newton Upper Falls, MA: Brookline Books.

Donnelly, Richard C. 1952. "Unconvicting the Innocent." *Vanderbilt Law Review* 6: 20.

Elliott, Robert G. 1940. *Agent of Death*. New York: E. P. Dutton.

Frank, Jerome, and Barbara Frank. 1957. *Not Guilty*. Garden City, NY: Doubleday.

Frankfurter, Felix. 1927. *The Case of Sacco and Vanzetti*. Boston: Little, Brown and Co.

Freedman, Eric M. 2002. *Habeas Corpus: Rethinking the Great Writ of Liberty*. New York: NYU Press.

Gardner, Earle Stanley, and William Sloane. 1952. *The Court of Last Resort*. New York: William Sloane Associates.

Gershman, Bennett L. 1992. "The New Prosecutors." *University of Pittsburgh Law Review* 53: 393, 451–54.

———. 1967. *Prosecutorial Misconduct*. Deerfield, IL: Clark Boardman Callaghan.

Givelber, Daniel. 1997. "Meaningless Acquittals, Meaningful Convictions: Do We Reliably Acquit the Innocent?" *Rutgers Law Review* 49: 1317.

Gross, Samuel L. 1998. "Lost Lives: Miscarriages of Justice in Capital Cases." *Law and Contemporary Problems* 61(4) (Autumn): 125–152.

———. 1996. "The Risks of Death: Why Erroneous Convictions Are Common in Capital Cases." *Buffalo Law Review* 44: 469.

Harris, Curtis. 2002. "The Courage of His Conviction." *City Limits: New York's Urban Affairs Magazine*, January.

Hirchberg, Max. 1940. "Convicting the Innocent," *Rocky Mountain Law Review* 13 (December): 20–46.

Huff, C. Ronald, Arye Rattner, and Edward Sagarin. 1996. *Convicted but Innocent: Wrongful Conviction and Public Policy*. Thousand Oaks, CA: Sage.

Humes, Edward. 1999. *Mean Justice*. New York: Simon and Schuster.

Inbau, Fred E., John E. Reid, and P. Buckley. 1986. *Criminal Interrogation and Confessions*. 3rd ed. Baltimore: Williams and Wilkins.

Kasdan, David S. 1985. "A Uniform Approach to New York State Liability for Wrongful Imprisonment" *Albany Law Review* 49: 201.

Klein, Henry H. 1927. *Sacrificed: The Story of Police Lieutenant Charles Becker*. New York: Isaac Goldmann Co.

Kunstler, William. 1960. *First Degree*. New York: Oceana Publications.

Lawes, Lewis E. 1940. *Meet the Murderer!* New York: Harper and Brothers.

Leo, Richard A., and R. J. Ofshe. 1998. "The Consequences of False Confessions: Deprivations of Liberty and Miscarriages of Justice in the Age of Psychological Interrogations." *Journal of Criminal Law and Criminology* 88: 429–96.

Loftus, Elizabeth. 1996. *Eyewitness Testimony*. Cambridge, MA: Harvard University Press.

Logan, Andy. 1970. *Against the Evidence: The Becker-Rosenthal Affair*. New York: McCall Publishing Co.

MacNamara, Donal E. J. 1969. "Convicting the Innocent." *Crime and Delinquency* 15 (January): 57–61.

McCloskey, James. 1989. "Convicting the Innocent." *Criminal Justice Ethics* 8 (Winter/Spring): 1–9.

National Commission on Law Observance and Enforcement. 1931. *Lawlessness in Law Enforcement.* Washington, DC.

O'Connor, Frank. 1974. "'That's the Man': A Sobering Study of Eyewitness Identification and the Polygraph." *St. John's Law Review* 49(1) (Fall): 1–30.

Penrod, Steven D. 1995. *Mistaken Identification: The Eyewitness, Psychology and the Law.* New York: Cambridge University Press.

Radelet, Michael L., Hugo Adam Bedau, and Constance E. Putnam. 1996. *In Spite of Innocence: Erroneous Convictions in Capital Cases.* Boston: Northeastern University Press.

Raab, Selwyn. 1967. *Justice in the Back Room.* Cleveland: World Publishing.

Radin, Edward D. 1964. *The Innocents.* New York: William Morrow.

Root, Jonathan. 1961. *One Night in July: The True Story of the Rosenthal-Becker Murder Case.* New York: Coward-McCann.

Rosenbaum, Martin I. 1990–91. "Inevitable Error: Wrongful New York State Homicide Convictions, 1965–1988." *New York University Review of Law and Social Change* 18: 807–30.

Scheck, Barry, Peter Neufeld, and Jim Dwyer. 2000. *Actual Innocence: When Justice Goes Wrong and How to Make It Right.* New York: Signet.

Smith, Abbe. 2000. "Defending the Innocent." *Connecticut Law Review* 32 (Winter): 485.

Squire, Amos. 1937. *Sing Sing Doctor.* Garden City, NY: Garden City Publishing Co.

Vick, Douglas W. 1995. "Poorhouse Justice: Underfunded Indigent Defense Services and Arbitrary Death Sentences." *Buffalo Law Review* 43: 329.

Wisotsky, Steven. 1997. "Miscarriages of Justice: Their Causes and Cures." *St. Thomas Law Review* 9: 547.

Yant, Martin. 1991. *Presumed Guilty: When Innocent People Are Wrongly Convicted.* Buffalo, NY: Prometheus Books.

Zimmerman, Isidore, with Francis Bond. 1964. *Punishment without Crime.* New York: Clarkson N. Potter.

Resources

The following not-for-profit organizations try to assist selected prisoners with their wrongful conviction cases.

Centurion Ministries
221 Witherspoon Street
Princeton, NJ 08542
http://www.centurionministries.org

DNA Forensic Testing Program—Oklahoma
1660 Cross Center Drive
Norman, OK 73019
(DNA cases in OK only)

The Innocence Project
Benjamin N. Cardozo School of Law
55 Fifth Avenue, 11th floor
New York, NY 10003-4391
http://www.innocenceproject.org
(DNA cases only)

Innocence Project Northwest
University of Washington School of Law
1100 NE Campus Parkway
Seattle, WA 98105-6617
http://www.ipnw.org
(WA, OR, AK, ID, and MT cases only)